P9-CBP-598

WITHDRAWN

FAMILY OF FAITH
LIBRARY

EFFECTIVE *Secondary School* DISCIPLINE

Every man who knows how to read has it in his power to magnify himself, to multiply the ways in which he exists, to make his life full, significant and interesting.

—ALDOUS HUXLEY

EFFECTIVE *Secondary School* DISCIPLINE

KNUTE G. LARSON
Principal, Cranston High School East
Cranston, Rhode Island;
Lecturer, Graduate Division
Rhode Island College
Providence, Rhode Island

MELVIN R. KARPAS
Professor of Educational Sociology
Chicago Teachers College South
Chicago, Illinois

PRENTICE-HALL, INC., Englewood Cliffs, N.J.

Second printing .... July, 1963

Library of Congress Catalog Card Number: 63-9967

Printed in the United States of America: 24582—B&P

TO OUR WIVES,
WHO HAD THE NECESSARY PATIENCE

ACKNOWLEDGMENT

To Dr. Bill Flanagan who came up with the idea and brought together the collaboration.

To George Horton, teacher-lecturer at Cranston High School East for invaluable editorial assistance.

Preface

Among the characteristics that make American public education unique perhaps the most significant are grass-roots control and grass-roots support. Over the years we have comfortably accepted local control of our schools although we have felt the pinch of local support. Also its unevenness has led to a wide disparity of quality.

The experience of our mushrooming suburbs has demonstrated that while America may worship bigness in industry, it is very reluctant to accept it in local government, even in the interest of efficiency. We cling tenaciously to our thousands of small, semi-independent school districts. Curiously, these districts are not diverse. They share common successes and failures in facing common problems. They have common goals and tend to watch each other very carefully.

This paradoxical uniformity was intensified during the period of renewal of interest in American education which followed the ascent of Sputnik I. The confusion and resentment following this achievement of Russian technology ushered in a period of rapid change and pure excitement in our schools. In a typically American fashion we milled around looking for a scapegoat and we found it in our public schools. Easily drawn to the sweeping generalization that seems to cut to the heart of a complex problem, America largely believed that:

1. The Russians had beaten us into space because they had more and better scientists.
2. They had the scientists because their schools concentrated on mathematics and science.

3. Russian schools worked children harder than ours and ignored frill courses and soft pedagogy.
4. Our secondary schools spend too much time on life-adjustment courses, fly-casting, and coeducational cooking at the expense of physics and mathematics.
5. Our high schools are ornate pleasure palaces full of lazy students and black-jacketed hoodlums.
6. Our schools are controlled by a tight clique of doctrinaire, anti-intellectual educationists.

Therefore, we should hasten to:

1. Turn the rascals out.
2. Make our schools more like the Russian schools.
3. Build bigger and better Sputniks.

It is fascinating to note that reports from Russia give us good reason to believe that the Red regime is far from satisfied with Russian education. Statements in Russian magazines lead us to believe that Anglo-American curriculum is being imitated behind the Iron Curtain. It would be the supreme irony of the century if we attempted to imitate the Russian schools at the very moment when they were attempting to imitate ours!

All of the criticism, just or unjust, concerns us deeply. One allegation that is particularly annoying is that discipline has deteriorated in our schools. This one hurts because it contains the seeds of truth—and the very community that points the finger at the schools makes it most difficult for the schools to take effective measures toward improvement.

The behavior of youth has always concerned the members of older generations. We can find words recorded as spoken by wise men going back to the dawn of history, words which state that the younger generation is inferior in many important respects to the older, that the young do not respect their elders. Perhaps society's elders will always feel this way.

How can we fairly describe the current status of discipline in our secondary schools? Discipline means different things to different people. To some it means a degree of submission to laws imposed by authority. To some it means lack of movement and noise. To others it means evidence of progress toward an acknowledged goal or purpose. In many cases it means a combination of some or all of these things.

In the first two decades of this century good discipline was almost universally thought of as unquestioned submission to authority. This was easy to administer in the high school because all but a handful of highly motivated, college-bound youth had dropped out of school before reaching this level. Expulsion was swift for the non-conformist unless his parents were influential in the community. That sometimes meant that a different set of standards existed for him.

With the third and fourth decades of the century came Progressive Education. The school's avowed emphasis became child-centered instead of book-centered; discipline was expected to come from within the child as a natural result of the powerful motivation to learning, the keynote of the new education. Eventually the pendulum began to swing the other way and children continued to grow in spite of shifts in educational philosophy. But too many words (some of them very funny) have been expended on second-guessing Progressive Education. It is sufficient to say that our public schools are undoubtedly better today because of the ferment created by this movement. John Dewey pointed the way toward *better* discipline, a strengthening of the controls of behavior within the child in the light of understood and accepted purpose. His was no advocacy of the anarchy that was sometimes perpetrated in his name by educational pygmies who followed the giant.

Soon after the dreary depression years, America was drawn into World War II. The steadying influence of the family was all but eliminated, with fathers away at war and mothers working in the factories. Nor did the post-war period with its ever-spiralling inflation help this situation. Great numbers of American mothers continued to work—although many of them found time to produce babies in fantastic numbers, compounding the problems of American education.

All of these factors combined with others to create great strains on our schools. Let us list some of these factors which affect secondary school discipline today, and bear in mind that it was not until after the time of Sputnik I that the American people were really aroused about their school to the point of effective action:

1. An ever rising birth rate since the close of World War II sharply increased our need for buildings and teachers. This strained severely the resources of the local taxpayer who had neglected his school buildings throughout the depression and war years. Crowded schools, too few properly trained teachers, and inadequate equipment do not combine to provide a proper atmosphere for good discipline.

2. Mass migration in and out of the cities and from region to region in our country further strained the facilities of our school systems in many areas as well as contributing to the adjustment problems of the uprooted youngsters.

3. America has accepted the policy of providing secondary school education for *all* American youth without providing the tools to accomplish this idealistic goal. Even today most of our secondary schools are not equipped to serve all the youth not better served by another type of institution. Faced with almost certain failure, maladjusted students who are required by law to attend school often seek an outlet for their frustration in aggressive and anti-social behavior.

4. Economic prosperity has brought with it an increased emphasis on doubtful values. The "big sell" of Madison Avenue

through the fantastic power of television has brainwashed millions of Americans into worshipping at the altar of a golden calf, and Moses seems to be nowhere in sight. The schools may try to teach one set of values but the student spends most of his life in a society that lives by a different set.

5. Technology has run away from man's social skills. Many of our youngsters drive 100 mph cars before they have been taught the meaning of responsibility. Yesterday's vandal painted cruel words on fences with a brush. Today's hoodlum uses a spray gun.

6. Increased tensions in today's world reflect themselves in increased conflicts in the adolescent's mind.

7. Amateurs with the best of intentions have plunged into youth work without adequate training or understanding, sometimes with sorry results.

8. Well-intentioned but naive people have pressured for an approach to juvenile delinquency which has resulted in overprotection.

America has deferred the status of adulthood for its youth to a questionable extreme. Other societies and other times have seen great responsibilities thrust upon young people. American history is rich with the heroic deeds of young men under 21 years of age. Positions of command involving life and death decisions have frequently gone to them in time of war. Yet today a softer society tries to prolong childhood and defer adulthood. This is unnatural and unwholesome, and its effects are felt in and out of school by those whose duty it is to teach discipline. Today the hardened young criminal belonging to that small group deterred from crime only by fear of punishment can operate almost with immunity. A kind society has limited severely the punishment which he may receive. He is frequently shocked at the age of 18 to discover that now he is to be held accountable for the same behavior which formerly resulted only in sympathetic lectures. This is patently unfair, both to society and to the individual.

The school has become an active, if unwilling, member of a team dealing with juvenile delinquency. Time after time the juvenile courts return the offenders to school. This action may be in the best interests of the individual involved but it places an unfair burden on the school. The principal has an obligation to protect his students from the influence of hardened criminals and perverts. Sometimes he is not permitted to do even this.

The secondary school today is a cross-section of the entire community, a slice of life. Its disciplinary tone reflects directly the tone of the adult community. It is, therefore, little wonder that the status of discipline in our secondary schools is not as favorable as it may have been in the past. In our larger cities these problems have been compounded by the presence of minority groups living in hellish slums and deprived of nearly all wholesome influences. It is indeed a tribute to the skills and dedication of our teachers, counselors, and administrators that we are doing as well as we are!

Introduction

This is a book of answers; it brings together some of the best contemporary thinking on the subject of secondary school discipline. It presumes to offer no easy panacea for these complicated problems but it does present practical and logical approaches which actually work in schools of all sizes in rural, suburban, and urban settings.

The authors speak from many years of experience as teachers and administrators in junior and senior high schools ranging in size from 90 to 3250 students. Their teaching and research have also been directed specifically at this problem in conducting graduate seminars on the subject. Out of the popularity of these seminars came a firm conviction of the need for this book. Graduate students have found much of the literature on school discipline to be repetitive and superficial. Much of it has been written by theorists. A bulk of the practical material has consisted of poorly edited cookbooks full of tasteless recipes. These induced a painstaking effort to collect the best material available, to combine it with the tested judgment of experience, and to present it in a logical manner.

Although the book is directed especially to the administrators and teachers of our junior and senior high schools, it also offers to parents, school board members, and to all youth workers an honest and non-technical picture of what our schools can do to solve the problems of discipline. A modest amount of theory, history, and philosophy is included where it is essential to a better understanding of the problems and the suggested solutions.

The book contains a basic review of step-by-step teaching

techniques for the beginning teacher and his supervisors because the authors are convinced that good teaching is the heart of good discipline. It concentrates on effective administrative policies and practices because a significant purpose of school administration is to provide a good learning and teaching atmosphere. It focuses attention on the community briefly because our schools can no longer exist in a vacuum but are tied directly to the community in which our youth live.

We have not written to point with pride, to view with alarm, or to grind any educational axe. We have summarized specific problems of secondary school discipline and presented specific approaches toward solutions—approaches which *have worked and continue to work* in American secondary schools.

Contents

1

Understanding Adolescents

It is not the intention of this volume to attempt to advance the frontiers of adolescent psychology, but rather to apply what we know now as a result of the efforts of scientists and the accumulated experience of generations of teachers. On the other hand, some preliminary consideration must be given to the nature of the adolescent and his growth problems in order that the teacher may plan effectively to treat diseases rather than symptoms in dealing with problems of disciplinary control. A logical starting point would seem to be: what are adolescents like, and what makes them misbehave?

Adolescence is the period of growth and change which takes place in the six or seven years between puberty and adulthood. Although there is a current reaction against emphasis on the turbulence and disequilibrium caused by the rapid and uneven growth of the adolescent, we cannot ignore these obvious phenomena when we try to understand him.

PROBLEMS FACING THE ADOLESCENT

The teacher comes to know the adolescent through his problems and his relative success in dealing with them. Let us consider some of these problems briefly in an attempt to understand his behavior.

1. The problem of understanding his body. All the abnormalities of rapid growth occur at a time when the adolescent is deeply concerned with being physically normal and attractive. Both boys and girls tend to become annoyed now and then by the amused tolerance with which their elders view the various phenomena of emerging adulthood. This apparent lack of understanding serves to create a gulf between many parents and their children. Teachers and administrators of secondary schools reduce their effectiveness sharply if they give youngsters the impression of patronizing amusement.

A very obvious physical phenomenon of adolescence is that girls begin to change sooner than boys and generally mature before the boys. This leads to a marked difference between the sexes in junior high school and makes it necessary to use different techniques in dealing with them in school. Many foreign school systems separate them completely during these years. American public schools do not. The remarkable thing is that so many teachers seem to ignore these differences completely. Differences between the sexes adjust themselves with the normal youngsters by the time they reach high school, but startling behavioral differences persist between maladjusted boys and girls, particularly in problems rooted in sex.

It is a matter of record that more boys than girls appear in juvenile courts. This is largely due to the fact that aggressive behavior is more common among boys than girls. This has led to the sensible practice of dual channeling by sexes of serious disciplinary referrals in many secondary schools. In larger schools it has led to the creation of offices of Dean of Boys and Dean of Girls.

2. The problem of relationships with other adolescents. What his peers think of him, or what he *thinks* they think of him, is a tremendous influence on the adolescent and cannot be lightly dismissed by teachers or parents. We consider this concern about peer attitudes to be one of the major causes of misbehavior. Later in this chapter we will point out and illustrate the implications of this fact in the need to work for the improvement of group values.

3. The problem of changing relationships with adults. The adolescent is like a bird that must try its wings. The mother bird can only keep him in the nest so long. Our society has shown a deplorable tendency to prolong dependence on adults and to filter the experiences of children. This delay of adulthood is also evident in many of the practices of secondary schools. Witness, for example, the common preoccupation with "covering" activities. How often are students permitted to do anything without the presence of a teacher? The justification for these precautions is usually based on legal responsibility, but we must remember that the practice conflicts with one of the basic needs of adolescence—the need for increased responsibility and independence in proportion to demonstrated maturity. Aren't we downgrading the youngsters by withholding these important rewards of adulthood?

Schools should plan carefully the extension of responsibilities and privileges to students so that by the time they reach high school they may enter a near-adult relationship with teachers and administrators. Certain obvious safeguards will always be necessary for those who have not matured and for those who have become maladjusted in the process, but there is little justification for treating groups of young adults as if they were still children.

4. The problem of communication with adults. Most adults are perplexed by adolescents, and most adolescents find it difficult to understand themselves. Yet they long for understanding. The major responsibility for maintaining lines of communication must remain with adults, especially teachers.

When a student has committed a foolish and trivial act

which has led to a private conference, the teacher will not usually get very far with a sharp-toned "Why did you do that?" A much better approach would be an oblique and friendly questioning on routine matters which can be easily and directly answered. Once a friendly atmosphere is established, the question of the specific foolishness can be raised if it has been demonstrated that anger is not involved.

5. The problem of economic independence and self respect. Another symptom of emerging adulthood is the need for some measure of financial independence and a full measure of self respect. The problem of allowances and part-time employment are largely the concern of parents, although many schools operate part-time employment services in connection with guidance. More than one problem youngster has been straightened out simply by getting him a part-time job. Schools operating work-experience programs wherein school credit is permitted for certain types of supervised employment during school hours, generally agree that the participating students seldom create discipline problems. In every case of part-time employment, however, the student must be made to realize that in case of conflict, his school responsibility comes first. It is particularly important to point out to parents and students that working to support an automobile cannot be justified if the student is having academic difficulty.

6. The problem of ideology and values. The disequilibrium of the adolescent frequently shows up in his political and religious views. He sometimes toys with iconoclasm, rejecting the views of his parents and experimenting with new ideas. There is no reason for alarm at this. It is the most natural thing in the world. All sorts of ideas should be open to him at this time and guidance need not be heavy handed in the direction of conformity.

When Johnny presents as his own an unorthodox and, perhaps, unpopular political viewpoint, he might well be asked to prepare to defend it against an equally prepared opposition from an able classmate at a future meeting of the class. Both students should be required to document their cases.

EARLIER RESEARCH INTO BEHAVIOR PROBLEMS OF ADOLESCENCE

Prior to World War II, the emphasis in research on citizenship development centered on hereditary and environmental factors such as intelligence, sex differences, the influence of peers and adults, and the impact of home environment.

The relationship of I.Q. to behavior patterns was a particularly popular subject for research. An intelligent youth obviously finds it easier to learn about desirable moral standards. He also learns more quickly about the unpleasant consequences of poor behavior. It does not follow that he will *choose* better behavior.

Studies of delinquency over several decades seem to indicate a greater amount of low intelligence and feeble-mindedness among children who get into serious trouble than among those who do not. This may be due in part to the greater ability of the intelligent children to understand values. (It may be also due to their greater ability to get away with misconduct!) Then, of course, there is the tendency of some dull children to express their frustration in anti-social behavior as a result of prolonged academic failure.

The influence of companions was not neglected in the earlier research on adolescent misbehavior. Much individual behavior was found to be group-linked, proving nothing in particular to teachers who had been aware of this as a result of their own observations.

The influence of the home was also found to be of tremendous importance. What parents say and do often shapes the behavioral pattern of the child beyond the power of the school or other institutions to change. Earlier studies all agreed on this point. This is not to say, however, that the influence of the school was written off completely. Schools which approached character and citizenship training directly and specifically were satisfied that the efforts were not in vain. Here the emphasis seemed to be on the nature of the pupil-teacher relationship and the strength of the teacher-image as a positive influence on the child. Too often teachers at all levels overestimate the power of other influences and underestimate what *they* can do. Secondary school students are not beyond hope when one remembers that they are actively *seeking* values at this period of their lives.

THE CONTEMPORARY APPROACH TO ADOLESCENT BEHAVIOR

Since World War II a change in emphasis has characterized causal studies into adolescent behavior. While earlier approaches have not necessarily been repudiated, a great deal of attention has recently been given to mental health. We turn more and more to the psychologist and psychiatrist for answers to problems of discipline in our schools. Teachers know that they must deal with groups of tremendously complicated individuals who will behave badly now and then in more or less normal reactions to frustrating conditions. They expect this and are prepared to deal with it because they know that proper behavior, like anything else, must be taught. They also know that among their groups of normally abnormal adolescents they will have to deal now and then with badly maladjusted personalities. They recognize that some of these should be referred to psychologists or psychiatrists, but they also know that in our society there are not enough of these specialists to go around. After a recommendation for referral, the teacher can only do her best to minimize further damage. When the welfare of the majority is seriously threatened she must recommend that the deviant be removed.

One of the results of this emphasis on mental health has been an increasing acceptance of the principle that tax money should be spent for services of this type. Psychological and even psychiatric services for public schools have, indeed, become increasingly available in recent years. The emphasis, however, has necessarily been on diagnosis and referral rather than treatment. The latter is still largely felt to be the responsibility of other agencies.

WHY DO YOUNGSTERS MISBEHAVE?

The Colonial schoolmaster was not too troubled with the causes of misbehavior. He had been taught that there was only one real cause—the presence of Satan in the child. He concerned himself with a cure which consisted mostly of physical purging of the Old Rascal. Later and more moderate interpretations were that there was a good deal of "natural mischief" in any child, particularly a boy, and a practical approach to discipline in school need not concern itself too much with the *why* of misbehavior. The real object should be the *how* of correction. We, too, shall concern ourselves with *how*, but the *why* must come first because it has a direct bearing on procedures.

In the light of what has been said above, let us attempt to list the major reasons for adolescent misbehavior in our secondary schools and consider briefly some ways to avoid them.

1. Confusion due to growth and change. We are asking the adolescent to sit quietly for rather long periods of time and to address himself to tasks which are not always pleasant and interesting. Often we fail to convince him that they are important to him. We cannot expect him to display constant patience and cooperation, with all of the exciting and perplexing things that are going on within him. His tasks require him to be logical and orderly. Nature urges him to be confused and bewildered.

The teacher should bear these things in mind and provide timely changes of pace and presentation to minimize the boredom that comes so easily to adolescents. The administrator should be guided accordingly in his schedule making, planning of lunch periods and recess, passing periods, etc., around the needs of students rather than solely for administrative convenience.

2. Confusion due to differing values. We have pointed out the natural tendency of the adolescent to experiment with values. This would cause enough trouble if he were living in a society with clear-cut and desirable values, but is he?

Today's adolescent lives in a confusing world. On every hand he is faced with double standards. He is taught to respect law and order and yet he sees evidences everywhere of crime and corruption. He is told to be tolerant and on every hand he sees intolerance. He is taught to respect humility and on every hand he sees aggressiveness and arrogance rewarded. All the media of communication bombard him with violence and brutality. It is significant that all of these seemingly powerful influences do not seem to lead the majority of our youth very far astray—only those who are weak. One wonders, on the other hand, what small influence they have on even those who are strong. Civilizations do not fall because of the complete corruption of a minority—they totter with the partial corruption of the majority.

3. Frustration due to fear. The adolescent is a worry wart. The things he worries about may seem trivial to an adult but they are real enough to him. Adults forget this when they speak of "carefree youth." The adolescent's boisterous laughter is often a facade presented to his companions because it is the thing to do. His schoolwork is often difficult for him. Most secondary schools, contrary to the opinions of critics who seem unaware of what is going on, *do* challenge their students. Enormous amounts of new and difficult material must be learned. The boy who worries because he has not learned to dance or the girl who fears that she will not be invited to the prom can be, for the moment, truly disturbed people. These fears may seem trivial to adults but they can lead to unpleasant consequences including poor grades and truancy.

The teacher can help her students minimize their fears by constant, friendly reassurance. When the symptoms become disturbing, referral should be made to the administration or the guidance department. It is precisely at a point like this that a trained counselor can be worth his weight in gold, but like a physician, he must be called upon before it is too late. As is true of any professional person, the teacher must know when to refer a problem to a specialist.

4. Frustration due to bad curriculum and poor teaching. A great many discipline problems are created by the school itself. Many of them can be eliminated once their existence has been honestly acknowledged and openly attacked.

5. Frustration due to societal injustices. A maladjusted individual will often rebel and strike back against the society which has hurt him. He is an angry individual. We also have in our society angry groups which have been offended by prejudice. We must be aware that many of our young people belong to minority groups which have been severely circumscribed in their choices. They find it difficult to enter certain trades and professions. Regardless of personal qualities or efforts, they are locked from birth into one class of society. Members of these groups must adjust to a lifetime of some degree of frustration no matter where they live. This cannot help but reflect itself in the behavior of some of them.

The individual teacher cannot overcome alone the injustices of society, but she can attempt to minimize further injustice in her own classroom. Here she has a strong influence on the atmosphere and can demonstrate her own faith in the American dream.

6. Influence of peers. We have pointed out that research and experience reveal the importance of the influence of companions on youth. Frequently the behavior of the individual is an index of the values of his group. If the school makes no effort to identify and to guide the *real* leaders of the student body they may have to deal with the questionable values of those who *assume* leadership. Students, like their elders, do not always elect the best qualified officers, but elections or, in some cases, appointments are to be preferred to self appointment.

One principal of a semi-rural high school was concerned with the clothing worn by the boys in his school. Dungarees had become popular around school and, as usually is the case, the boys began to behave as poorly as they dressed.

Not wishing to precipitate a crisis, the principal called together a group of boys whom he considered to be the real leaders of the school and talked with them about the problem. He pointed out that visitors would get a poor impression of the school if boys wore dungarees to classes, and also frankly spoke of the correlation between good clothes and good manners. Then he opened the matter up for discussion. Minor points were cleared up and it was agreed to debate the issue in a "town meeting" assembly. The principal agreed that even if the students voted to abolish dungarees, an individual could wear them if his reasons were sound and if one of his parents appeared to justify the privilege. He knew that there was little chance of this happening if the majority were to reject dungarees.

The students held their meeting after a brief period of campaigning pro and con. In a secret ballot they voted overwhelmingly against dungarees, and they disappeared from the school.

The lesson learned in this incident was that *peer group*

values could be upgraded if handled patiently and democratically. It seems rather obvious that if students behave poorly because of bad group patterns, they will improve if the patterns improve. Poor group values usually exist only because true leadership has not been identified and guided. This is the principal's task. He can also utilize his leadership in assemblies by frequent short appeals to group spirit and pride in the school. If this is done with skill and without overtones of preaching it can be most effective.

The teacher can also take peer group influence into account by not insisting that the student violate the code in minor matters. It is unfair, for example, to ask any secondary school student to inform on another one in cases of petty misdemeanors. If the offense is serious, this is another matter and should be handled by the principal. There is no excuse for perpetuating a criminal code, but there is no point either in forcing a difficult decision on an adolescent when the matter can be handled in another way.

7. Influence of adult examples. Students sometimes behave poorly in imitation of adults. They are told to respect the law. They see their parents and other adults fixing traffic tickets and openly conspiring to cheat on income taxes. All this is happening at an impressionable age. Teachers and administrators can point out to students that they must create their own values and not be influenced by the weaknesses of others, young or old. They must learn not to expect perfection in adults they admire. This is the time when they can begin to learn that the greatness of some of history's most heroic figures was not obliterated by their human weaknesses. Adolescence is the time to begin to overcome the tendency of the youngster to look at life in terms of white and black, and to reject the child-oriented western with its clean-cut heroes and its villains, identifiable by black hats and mustaches.

8. **Influence of poor home conditions.** Teachers often find that students who habitually misbehave do not come from completely happy homes. Court authorities agree that broken or tension-filled homes accompany a good deal of juvenile delinquency. We have pointed out the inference of the earlier studies that the important factor in bad homes was the poor example set by adults. The recent emphasis is on the poor emotional climate on bad home environment. In either case the school faces a tremendous problem. Educators do not agree on the extent of the school's responsibility or legal right to work directly in improving these conditions, but the traditional truant officer has been largely replaced by a trained social worker who does involve himself to some extent in the affairs of the home when the welfare of the child is threatened or prior to court action. Proper guidance and a wholesome school atmosphere can help a great deal in overcoming the influence of poor home conditions, but it is usually an uphill struggle. If the roots of the difficulty are to be reached and if the child's welfare is really being threatened, some agency should get into the home and help the family in solving its problems. On the other hand, the sanctity of the home should not be violated lightly by overeager officialdom. In any event, there is always hope for improvement once we know what we are dealing with.

RECOMMENDATIONS FOR ADMINISTRATORS

Principals have become increasingly aware of staff weaknesses in knowledge of adolescent psychology, and in the application of this knowledge. Perhaps it is due to an overemphasis on theory in our colleges. Perhaps it is due to a lack of understanding or an unwillingness on the part of teachers to apply what they have learned for fear that it is not truly applicable. Whatever the reason, the result is too often a condition which contributes to poor discipline. Principals can help to improve this situation by direct action. Here are some suggestions:

1. Obtain books and other materials for beginning teachers which call attention to the characteristics of adolescence and point out applications, preferably by illustrative anecdotes. The readings should be required and followed by discussions as part of the orientation of new teachers. It would not do any harm to make this material available to *all* teachers.

2. The principal may prefer to prepare his own suggestions, perhaps with the assistance of members of the staff. This need not be an overwhelming task and it could result in material that is pertinent and useful.

3. Specialists should be brought in for in-service courses and conferences. Every effort should be made to obtain speakers thoroughly grounded in classroom teaching. Teachers weary quickly of lectures on theory by theoreticians.

4. Teachers should be encouraged to visit superior schools and superior teachers. Visiting days with pay are a common policy these days, but many teachers fail to take advantage of them—particularly the teachers who could profit most. It is the responsibility of the principal to encourage visitation and to recommend schools to be visited. A follow-up in the form of a brief report at a faculty meeting should be a normal sequel to such a visit.

5. Teachers who seem to experience difficulties in getting along with certain students should be invited to conferences in which guidance counselors and administrators discuss the problems of these students. Often this practice leads to amazing improvements simply by pooling information and suggestions.

The basic principle to be borne in mind is that knowledge about adolescence does not always insure teacher action consonant with that knowledge. As is the case with students, transfer of training from theory to action must often be brought about by specific and pointed directions and illustrations. The leadership in this continuing program of teacher training must come from administrators whose main function is, after all, to improve the quality of instruction and to bring about conditions conducive to learning.

2

A Vital Curriculum as Basic to Good Discipline

Curriculum, like most educational terms, has a variety of meanings. For our purposes we can think of the curriculum as the sum of all the purposeful experiences the student is exposed to and over which the school has control. From the viewpoint of this definition one can readily see that the quality of the curriculum can influence to a great degree the disciplinary tone of the school.

WHERE ARE WE?

American secondary schools faced their greatest challenge at mid-century. Buffeted by conflicting pressures for three centuries; subjected to alternating periods of brief concern and lengthier neglect; undermined by widespread mediocrity in staff, equipment, and plant; and prodded by a bitter wave of criticism, they faced the task of providing quality education for unprecedented numbers of children.

In spite of all these handicaps and in spite of their historic resistance to change our schools did respond to the stimulus of public attention and support, but sweeping changes in public institutions are not effected overnight. In the meantime millions of youngsters are passing through our junior and senior high schools.

It is perfectly understandable that the individual child does not always find answers to his personal needs in such a vast undertaking. If he plans to go on to college, he is more fortunate than those who do not, because most American secondary schools still place the greatest emphasis on college preparation. On the other hand, he frequently finds himself shackled by the sequence of courses which may have little relationship to the type of college he wants to attend. His science courses may be designed as preparation for students who will major in science. His math may be taught as a preparation for engineering, whereas he may be interested primarily in the humanities. He may be forced to study a language in which he can and will find only the vaguest value. His entire sequence may have been designed to meet the college entrance requirements of his grandfather's day.

In addition to this, he often finds himself in classes too large and too varied in ability for the teacher to give him the attention he needs. Consequently, teaching is aimed at the middle group, which may be too fast or too slow for him. Sooner or later he will be either confused or bored.

Even if our student attends a small school, he soon feels the impact of bigness and impersonality in education. He is bombarded with examinations designed and produced by large outside organizations, covering material which may or may not have been adequately covered in his classes. Using the results of these examinations, a machine which punches holes in a card classifies him, and these holes may determine his whole future. He cannot help but feel akin to the recruits who stand naked in a drafty examination room with hundreds of others, having data painted on their hides with merthiolate. He is, in short, being robbed of one of the most precious rights of an American—the right to maintain his dignity as an individual.

The student who does not plan to go on to college also shares this loss of individuality. To make matters worse for him, he finds that the very courses which have the most meaning for him are either unavailable or are grudgingly offered in the fringes of the curriculum. His academic courses may be watered-down versions of the college-preparatory curriculum, still taught with a heavy emphasis on the textbook. His status in the school is stigmatized by his classification as a *general, industrial arts,* or *comprehensive* student. This appears on his records, his report cards, and sometimes on his diploma. He cannot even chuck the whole business in favor of going to work until he is sixteen and then only with his parents' permission. Is it any wonder that he sometimes rebels against such an atmosphere?

HOW DID WE GET THIS WAY?

We have pointed out that American schools are creatures of the American people. This generalization is, of course, subject to the qualification that only a small percentage of our people know enough or care enough about our schools to exert any influence on them. Schools, like all democratic institutions, are subject to pressures. The curriculum of our secondary schools is a product of many of these pressures exerted over the past three centuries. Sometimes these pressures have moved in conflcting directions. Sometimes they have moved in concert. Future changes can only grow out of an understanding of the past. Let us, therefore, review briefly some of these important influences:

1. Tradition and history. Our first secondary schools were created to help supply needed professional men, particularly clergymen, for the early colonies. The curriculum was almost entirely classical in the European tradition. Over the years other pressures were felt, faintly at first, to provide a more practical curriculum. Benjamin Franklin, the unparalleled genius of our young nation, spoke out for a curriculum that would be both "useful and ornamental," but the influence of the classicists persisted and still persists to some degree today. The reasons for this, over and above the power of tradition itself, are something like these: (a) Truth is eternal and great values never change. Since the greatest truths found their optimum expression in the culture of the classical period, truly educated men must learn the languages of this period to unlock this culture. (b) The significant culture of the subsequent periods was largely created by men educated in the classical tradition and cannot be appreciated without an adequate indoctrination in the same milieu. (c) Classical languages form a foundation for a mastery of our own and other modern languages. (d) Classical languages are difficult to learn and their mastery trains the mind for other tasks.

A moderation of this emphasis finally came after a half century of psychological research refuted argument (d) with a mountain of evidence that the mind cannot be trained like a muscle, and that the amount of transfer from one situation to another is too slight to justify learning anything simply for the sake of transfer. Latin has survived, but now it must stand on its own feet. It does provide a valuable foundation for those who intend further language study and it provides a key to the understanding and appreciation of later art forms, notably the literature of 18th and 19th century England. The difference is that now it has lost most of its cloak of special privilege and must compete with other subjects. Greek, as a subject of study in public secondary schools, is largely dead.

Although many teachers are still convinced that it doesn't matter what you study as long as it is difficult, the scientific refutation of transfer of training has also forced other subjects to compete in the open market. One can easily see the relationship between traditionalism and school discipline. Overdoses of abstract, difficult material of dubious value encourage many students to seek refuge in daydreaming, truancy, and overt misbehavior.

2. The shadow of Calvinism. The Puritan doctrines have found themselves tempered by three centuries of relative enlightenment, but they have not lost their grip on New England, and the influence of New England is still felt in varying degrees all over America. Soft drinks are still called "tonic" in Boston. The pleasant tasting stuff still plagues the New England conscience, which relieves itself by giving it a medicinal name. This undertone of fire and brimstone still has its hold on the curriculum of America's public schools. Our collective conscience, still influenced by Calvin's dour doctrines, stirs uneasily at the thought of anything too pleasant going on in the schools.

3. The college influence. Secondary schools have always been very sensitive to the requirements, real or fancied, of colleges. Frequently, all students who plan to obtain some kind of post-high school education are grouped together in a sequence of courses designed to meet the requirements of the most demanding colleges. Small high schools often feel that this is necessary in order to provide reasonable class sizes in the advanced courses. The trouble is that many of these students have neither the need nor the ability for some of this work, especially at the twelfth grade level. The result is either failure for some or a lowering of standards for all. The girl who plans to enter a three-year nursing school must frequently choose between programs that will not prepare her for admission or which will take her far beyond the requirements.

Another problem which accompanies the two-track, college and non-college curriculum is that of social prestige. Many youngsters choose the college preparatory program simply because of the stigma attached to the other alternatives. This intensifies the problems of the school, since many of these students could do superior work in courses geared to their abilities. Their presence would, in fact, strengthen these courses. Instead they create problems for teachers in college preparatory courses who have no desire to fail wholesale numbers. The net result of this mass unwillingness to face reality, especially in the larger schools, is a *pseudo*-college preparatory program, wherein inappropriate materials are pabulummed to satisfy the prestige needs of students and parents. Fortunately, it is possible to offer some useful courses to this group, since their limitations usually prevent them from pursuing some of their required courses beyond two years. After having searched for one or two years for the secret of the cipher, they drop their foreign language. That makes room for a more useful course.

Many educators have expressed the opinion that the solution for this problem lies in the removal of the offensive labels and individualization of all programs. In this way students may still be grouped for effective preparatory work, but there will be no need to select courses merely for the prestige value of titles. This may be true but changes of this sort come about slowly in our high schools. Often the fear of lowering standards prevents changes which would actually raise them.

4. Pressure groups. The curriculum of our secondary schools is also influenced by the good intentions of pressure groups; for example, patriotic organizations, and various foundations which, when providing funds for educational improvements, cannot resist the temptation to influence curriculum by various emphases which conform with the prejudices of important officials of the foundation itself. Usually these groups are after a better understanding of our heritage or improved educational practices. These are most desirable goals, but need not always be realized by merely adding courses with appropriate titles or by stressing one side of controversial issues.

Minority groups also make their presence felt. Sometimes obscure foreign languages are taught in high schools because of the political influence of vociferous groups in the community and without regard for the relative importance of the literature or culture represented.

Social studies materials are particularly vulnerable to the efforts of pressure groups. This frequently results in weak, washed-out textbooks, which may not offend any group but which also fail to interest many students. Dull textbooks are, indeed, the root of many disciplinary problems. This is due not so much to the inept handling of difficult concepts, but rather to the skill some writers seem to have in converting the most fascinating material into bland, unsavory stuff. Many teachers adopt a defeatist attitude about poor texts and simply go along with them year after year instead of making their opinions felt in the right places, and by supplementing them with lively materials which are easy enough to obtain with a little effort.

5. Bandwagons. In spite of their basically conservative nature, the public schools respond to important movements and events. Progressive education of the twenties and thirties was such a movement, and its influence was certainly felt in the lower elementary school. Who can ignore the bandwagon effect of Sputnik I on our schools? The resultant wave of criticism and soul searching has had a profound effect on our junior and senior high school curriculum. The tremendously influential Conant reports on our junior and senior high schools have almost become standard procedural guides for American secondary education. The powerful College Entrance Examination Board, too, has made itself felt in the high schools.

The trouble with these sporadic movements is that they tend, in some schools, to cause too rapid shifting of gears from extreme lethargy to hasty changes. *Curriculum development should be an orderly and constant process.* Rapid, extensive changes lead to widespread feelings of insecurity to teachers.

This inevitably influences students and leads to restlessness and poor morale.

Students, too, are tempted by bandwagons. One of the effects of the shift of emphasis to math and science was a widespread interest in physics and chemistry by students with limited academic ability. There would have been no problem if these young people had been satisfied with courses geared to their limitations, but many of them saw themselves as potential scientists rather than as potential automobile mechanics. Under these conditions, disappointment was almost inevitable, for only a certain percentage of our youth has the ability, interest, and determination to achieve college level work in science. The mere need for more scientists does not change that percentage. Perhaps we could have concentrated some of our propaganda efforts on the need for lower level technicians as well as top scientists. The encouragement of unattainable goals leads to disappointment, discontentment, and bad behavior.

6. Local school boards. The policy-making bodies of our public schools are frequently the least influential in matters of curriculum except as they reflect the pressures mentioned above. Often they concern themselves chiefly with the trivia of administration, leaving the real meat of education to hirelings.

These, then, are the chief influences exerted on the school curriculum: tradition and history; the shadow of Calvinism; the college influence; pressure groups; bandwagons; and school boards. They are the forces that caused us to "get this way." We seem to be in general agreement as to the nature of our curriculum deficiences. We agree that these inadequacies cause discipline problems with students who fail to find real meaning in their school work. Where we fail to agree is in how to go about remedying this situation. The cure is not simple and involves various organizational modifications in our schools as well as specific changes in the nature and sequence of offerings.

Many attempts have been made to effect these changes. Some of them show great promise.

The following is an attempt to point out some of the more promising developments which have been successful in improving the programs of secondary schools and thus make education more meaningful for youngsters. Detailed descriptions of all of them are readily available from the NEA, the federal and state departments of education, university libraries, etc. While it is perfectly true that a given program may succeed in one school and fail in another, it is also reasonable to expect any school system to be aware of changes taking place all over the country and to assign able staff members to an open-minded study of these changes.

WHERE DO WE GO FROM HERE?

Some of the more interesting experiments have to do with staff utilization. There is growing evidence that the use of teams of teachers with diverse responsibilities and appropriate pay differentials can lead to more effective instruction. Experiments with large and small group teaching have also proven extremely interesting. Flexibility in class size seems to be particularly promising as an approach to meeting individual needs. Large group instruction has been very effective for high ability students, but the experience of the writers leads to a cautious view of the claim that it can be used for all ability levels.

Another organizational change which promises a general improvement in the quality of education is the widespread trend to consolidate small school districts. This has become particularly popular as a way to provide a better secondary education. Consolidation usually leads to more state aid which, in turn, may buy a better program. America's small, rural high schools may lay claim to a better record in discipline than her city schools, but the real reason for this is usually found in an extremely high drop-out rate in the rural schools. Students who leave because they feel there is nothing for them in the schools create no further discipline problems, but they may have limited sharply their usefulness to society.

Closely allied to consolidation is the increased emphasis on the sharing of resources, facilities, and personnel. Guidance facilities and counselors are now available to many small schools on the part-time basis through country, state, and other cooperative agencies. Psychiatric services, for example, can be made available in this way. Small schools have found that it is far better to obtain the services of trained specialists for one or two days a week than it is to lighten the load of a teacher and expect him to become trained in a given specialty. A full time specialist is almost always more effective than a jack-of-all-trades.

CURRICULUM CHANGES

The pace of curriculum improvement accelerated greatly in the late fifties and early sixties. Some of the resultant changes led into blind alleys but most of them made good sense. The overall effectiveness of any change in education depends largely on the classroom teacher. We intend to develop this important point in a later chapter and show how this relates itself to good discipline. For the moment, we shall concern ourselves briefly with the changes themselves—changes which can lead to better discipline simply because a student who is being skillfully taught significant material will rarely misbehave badly.

One of the most frequently voiced complaints about our secondary schools is that they do not challenge sufficiently our gifted students. Every school has tried to solve this problem in a variety of ways. The difference in the post-Sputnik years was in the advantages of a nationwide crash program. Whereas in the past, parents had resisted the efforts of the schools to increase the work loads of able youngsters, now public sentiment made it almost un-American not to do so. A tendency became apparent to identify these youngsters as early as possible, and to group them for a special program with greater depth and speed. We failed to reach much agreement on the nature of this program or even on the definition of such terms as *acceleration* and *enrichment,* but the net effect was an increased workload for students and for teachers. At first the results were uneven, but where the quality as well as the quantity of the work was stepped up, excellent results were obtained.

Less attention at first was paid to the other side of the coin—challenging the academically handicapped students to work up to the limits of their abilities. With an increase of coordination between elementary and secondary schools that came with the stepped-up emphasis on curriculum improvement, effective measures began to appear in better school systems. Slow learners were grouped by ability in reading in elementary schools and intensive efforts were directed to improving their skills. Secondary schools began to do something about truly accepting these students *where they were* educationally and providing appropriate instruction for them even when it meant starting at a very low level. This dual approach to the problem of the slower learners (persistent application of appropriate teaching and realistic grouping by reading ability) began to pay off where it was given an honest effort.

Following the publication of Conant's *The American High School Today,* homogeneous grouping increased in popularity. While there was still confusion as to what really constituted homogeneity in this context, there was little doubt that teachers were pleased with an attempt to obtain it. Intelligently administered, this form of grouping had undeniable advantages in some courses. Like any device, it can be overdone, but along with a renewal of interest in grouping followed another sound emphasis—a new look at individual differences, which is perhaps the true Achilles' Heel of American education. More words and less action have been expended on this than on any other facet of education in our nation. The right of the individual to be different and to have his individuality respected goes beyond the educational scene to the very heart of our national purpose. Here is something that makes democracy superior to other political systems. It seems elementary that we should devote a good deal of thought to it in our curriculum planning and in our methods of teaching.

Modern languages. Following World War II, a revolution began to take place in the teaching of modern foreign languages. The armed forces had discovered during World War II that very few Americans could use foreign languages effectively, especially such languages as Japanese, Chinese, and Russian. People who had studied various foreign languages in school could not converse easily in them because their learning had been aimed mostly at a reading and translating knowledge rather than at speaking and listening skills. Faced with the need for thousands of people who could speak and understand various languages, the armed forces instituted a crash program which seemed to have remarkable results. A minimum of effort was expended in teaching formal grammar and the emphasis was placed on talking and listening. Later this became known as the oral-aural approach to language study.

When America really awakened to the need for language study in the fifties, exciting things began to happen. Language study was moved down into the junior high school in many communities and, in some cases into the lower elementary grades. Dabbling in languages was discouraged, and students were urged to carry one language to mastery. The oral-aural approach was stressed, at least in the early stages, and language laboratories made available electronically the voices of natives speaking the various tongues. The world situation also encouraged the introduction of Russian and other neglected languages into the curriculum of some schools. The net result of all this change was to make language study far more interesting to the students.

Mathematics. This period of change also saw something of a revolution in mathematics, led not by public school educators but by scholars in the field. The term *new mathematics* became the storm center of a controversy. Proponents of change claimed that conventional math as it was taught in secondary schools placed too much emphasis on the superficial manipulation of figures. What was needed, they claimed, was a deeper understanding of basic principles. More conservative observers claimed that this reasoning went too far away from scientific applications of mathematics into an area fit only for abstract thinkers. They felt that the real basis of math should be in its links with science and that the trouble in high schools stemmed from poor teaching rather than poor courses of study. At any rate, the mathematical pot was set to bubbling.

English. English has always been under fire in secondary schools. Students resist the teaching of the mechanics of English more effectively than any other subject. Perhaps this is due to the fact that they can practice poor English in daily living, but poor mathematics will cost them money. In adolescent society, the use of good grammar in conversation is frowned upon.

A large scale change in the English program during this period of curriculum revolution was a sharply increased emphasis on the tools of communication. Many administrators felt that underdeveloped reading ability was the greatest cause of discipline trouble resulting from academic frustration in our secondary schools. Formal reading instruction began to appear right up through the high school in the forms of remedial reading, developmental reading, and reading acceleration. Large pupil loads had prevented most English teachers from assigning very much written work, especially in the high schools.

Various devices such as hiring educated housewives to correct papers were attempted, but it became clear that the only effective way to get more written work out of students was to cut the teaching load of English teachers and to strengthen supervision in this field.

Social studies. Even social studies finally received some attention in the wake of Sputnik I. Extensive duplication was revealed throughout the grades in some phases, and a great deal of important material became conspicuous by its absence. A great emphasis had always been placed on the study of Western Europe and America, and almost completely ignored were the history and geography of South America, Asia, and Africa, except as they were affected by the United States and the nations of Western Europe. A revival of interest in the teaching of citizenship skills for slow learners also followed. Courses such as *Problems of Democracy* began to take on a new look with a beneficial effect on the general tone of morale and discipline among the students involved. We have pointed out that discipline, like anything else in school life, must be taught, and no place more logical can be found to teach it than in courses like the following:

Science. Secondary school science received, of course, a lion's share of everyone's attention. College professors claimed that the high schools needed to reorganize their offerings, particularly in physics where so much new material had to be mastered every year. They pointed out that the engineering applications commonly stressed in high school physics should be moved back into junior high school to make room for a greater emphasis on nuclear physics. As did the mathematicians, they urged the high school teachers to return to college and master the new material. Many high school teachers believed that the college people did not have a very realistic idea of how many high school students were able to master material of this type.

Science curriculum committees, like their colleagues in other fields, found plenty of room for improvement, especially in the offerings for the very able and for the very slow learners. As we have stated, these are critical spots for discipline trouble. Boredom rests at one extreme and frustration at the other.

The arts. As is usual, the arts felt the pinch of the tightening process. The increased demands in the basic subjects made it difficult for serious college preparatory students to elect subjects such as art and music. Teachers in these fields resented this renewal of the implication that the arts are a fringe area in education—a nice kind of therapy for the maladjusted and a time consumer for the slow learner, but hardly worth the serious efforts of bright students. They renewed their battle for a place in the educational sun and efforts were made through schedule adjustments to alleviate the situation. A most desirable result of study by curriculum committees in art and music was a shift in emphasis away from performance to appreciation. Music in some schools had meant only marching bands. Now it also began to include education for intelligent listening and a richer life through appreciation of fine music. Similarly, art classes began to learn about viewing rather than doing.

Part of the reason for these subjects being under suspicion within the schools themselves is the feeling of some teachers that students are being entertained rather than educated when they elect art or music. Academic teachers, particularly the stuffier ones, harbor the suspicion that anyone can teach students to look at paintings and listen to music, and that the whole undertaking is only a step removed from a vaudeville show. Needless to say, the most active of these critics are seldom seen visiting classes in art and music appreciation. "Music hath charms to sooth the savage breast" even when that breast is cloaked in a black leather jacket!

Physical education. One phase of school work which did not require a Russian bugle call to expose its inadequacies was physical education. The accumulated evidence of World War II and the Korean War was more than enough to convince America that her young men were incredibly soft in comparison with the youth of other nations. Too much material prosperity seemed to have taken its toll. Military leaders and even Presidents Eisenhower and Kennedy asked for more rigorous conditioning of body and spirit for our youth. Slowly but certainly our schools began to respond with a more demanding program of physical education. The number of periods per week was increased and more rigorous activities were required. Parental resistance appeared as a result of the complaints of their offspring, but a new spirit was in the air in response to the challenge of a new crisis. This seemed to bear out the theory that American youth had been behaving badly because it had been spoiled with too much soft living. Lacking the feeling of crisis that had been provided by past depression and wars, it had degenerated into an aimless softness which resulted in unintelligent rebellion against society. Perhaps it is an oversimplification of a complicated problem to submit that lack of crisis begets flabby living and flabby morals, but it does tie in rather neatly with the ancient idea that the Devil finds work for idle hands. It would certainly be difficult to prove that school discipline would be adversely affected by a more demanding physical education program.

Citizenship development. America's basically negative role in the cold war underscored the need for a positive indoctrination of our youth. They needed, of course, to understand Communism and why we were opposed to it, but they also needed a better understanding of what democracy was all about. Critical studies led us again to the importance of participation —of learning by doing. Citizenship programs involving student participation in real situations such as working for political parties in actual elections, had been attempted here and there over several decades, but they never received widespread support. At best, they were thought of as desirable extras. Now they began to receive attention again, at least in the professional literature.

Work-experience programs. The integration of school and work has long played a minor role in American secondary education. Here and there it has received enthusiastic support for many years, particularly in the field of commercial education. In 1957, Cranston High School East in Cranston, Rhode Island, expanded its work-experience program to include the training of nurses' aides in cooperation with the Rhode Island Hospital and the Osteopathic Hospital of Cranston. The girls in this program alternated two weeks of related academic work in school with two weeks of training and experience at the hospitals. After three years of operation, the school reached four interesting conclusions about this program: (1) not one girl participating in the program had dropped out before graduation, (2) not one girl in the program had been involved in a disciplinary referral to the administration, (3) every girl in the program had matured perceptibly faster than nonparticipating classmates, and (4) a great majority of the program's graduates had gone into some form of hospital or related employment.

This school had similar experiences with its cooperative retailing program operated over a decade with a large department store. Many inferences have been drawn from these experiences, some of which may be subject to challenge. Two facts, however, seem beyond dispute. There has been no disciplinary trouble worthy of the name in connection with any student in either cooperative program; and the combination of real job experience with related school work has all but eliminated lack of meaning from the curriculum of these students.

One conclusion is simple. Discipline trouble often is a result of a curriculum that simply doesn't make sense to students. Meaning or purpose in a curriculum has little relationship to the relative academic difficulty of the courses. Continued study of the curriculum in relation to the real needs of students, by teachers involved in the actual classroom process, is a very important factor in maintaining good discipline in our secondary schools.

3

The Effective Lesson Comes First

Above all, the principal should be an instructional leader. The only significant purpose of educational administration and supervision is helping teachers to do a better job of teaching. In his classroom visitations and ensuing conferences, in his staff meetings, and through his work with subordinate administrators, the principal is responsible for the constant improvement of instruction, and through it the disciplinary tone of the school.

The principal of any but the smallest school must be relieved from teaching assignments of his own in order properly to conduct his work. Once relieved, however, he begins his long climb into the administrative tower, away from the day-to-day aspects of classroom teaching. He needs to be reminded, in ways more forceful than rear-seat visits, of the teacher's problems and the classroom point of view. This chapter is intended to serve as a reminder, a brief review of what is expected of the teacher and how he can be helped in achieving it.

THE CLASSROOM TEACHER

Discipline in the classroom is not an entity in itself, it is a product of good teaching, and staff and administrative teamwork. The classroom teacher, as he greets his first class in September, stands second in importance in the lives of his students only to their parents. It hardly seems necessary to dwell on the significance of what he says and does at that moment. On the other hand, it might be interesting to consider briefly just what is expected of him. What is he *supposed* to do? What steps have been taken to see that he will be able to do it?

The answers are not simple. Different people expect different things of him. Most of the young people waiting for him to speak expect, in varying degrees, the same general things of him. They expect him, first of all, to be a nice guy. Not that they want him to run in a popularity contest, but they do want to like him, and they want him to like them.

They expect him to make them *want* to learn his subject. They expect him to prove to them that it will be useful to them in a way they can understand. They expect him to generate enthusiasm. They want his classes to be *alive*. They have all had liberal doses of boredom in the past and they want no more of it. They expect him to be skillful and understanding so that learning can come to them as easily as possible. They expect him to be both patient and demanding, for they know in their hearts that anything worth having is difficult to attain. They want him to respect them for what they are and, most of all, for what they can become. They want very much to respect *him*. A few of these youngsters, of course, expect too much. The best teacher will not be able to reach them. This is perfectly normal and should not discourage him.

Their parents expect even more of him. They expect him to set standards for their children that they themselves frequently have been unable to set. They expect him somehow to hasten the process of maturing. Some of them even expect him to develop talents that do not exist.

His administrators expect a great deal too. They believe that he should try to develop to the maximum the measured potential of all his students. They expect good classroom order which they do not measure merely in terms of absence of noise. They expect cooperation and loyalty but not subservience. They expect him to be interested in the problems of the individual without losing sight of his responsibilities to the group. They expect that his teaching function will maintain the highest priority. They did not hire him to become an amateur psychiatrist nor a detention-home guard.

It would seem, then, that a great deal is expected of our classroom teacher. One might even say that he is expected to perform a series of miracles; not big miracles, but little miracles like the fine performance of a violin virtuoso; little miracles that are produced every day through a combination of intelligence, talent, and HARD WORK.

It has been somewhat cynically suggested that only ten percent of the people in any line of work really know what they are doing. Perhaps this is a cruel underestimation of man's capacity and willingness to perform, but we do know that truly effective teachers are all too scarce. To pretend otherwise is to shut our eyes to overwhelming evidence.

We have said that fine teaching consists of a series of small miracles like those performed every day in other fields by people who truly care about their work. This is not to say that every teacher can perform them every day. The important thing is to know what causes these miracles. The basic ingredients have been suggested—intelligence, talent, and hard work. The proportions will vary with the individual. Let us examine briefly each of these ingredients as it relates itself to the classroom performance.

The term *intelligence* covers a great deal of territory, some of it yet unexplored, but we have reached an area of agreement that permits us to use the term as a tool in dealing with children. Apply this same general meaning to the teacher. He should have an alert and open mind, a quick wit, and a ready imagination. He should have a solid academic preparation with a healthy major in his subject area, buttressed with a continuing lively interest that leads to constant reading in his field. He should have an adequate preparation in the skills of pedagogy and a knowledge of the ground rules and policies of his particular school. Weaknesses in subject matter and/or pedagogy can sometimes be corrected with more hard work. Even the most successful teachers feel a need to learn more about their specialties. We cannot expect the beginner to have all the answers.

Talent, too, can be an elusive term. The outstanding teacher is usually part actor. Teaching inevitably involves salesmanship. Call it professional enthusiasm if you prefer, but we do know that an effective teacher gives off sparks. He is dynamic. He generates enthusiasm to others. Some of this may be acquired but most of it is there when the future teacher emits his first howl as a result of the doctor's well-aimed slap. A good teacher should have a personality that permits:

1. A sincere liking of people. This seems obvious, yet it is not too difficult to find teachers whose every action points to a dislike for kids. Why are they teaching? There are so many other ways to make a living.
2. The acceptance of many points of view. Tolerance is not enough. Pupils come from unbelievably different backgrounds. We cannot guide them into our world unless we understand theirs.
3. A willingness to be a "take charge" person. The much needed revolt of the Progressive era against authoritarian teaching took some of us a bit too far away from some very practical considerations. The teacher must have a steady hand on the tiller if the boat is to move toward a fixed destination, and like a good officer, must be able to state a direction, com-

mand, or request as if he *expects* it to be followed. Democratic participation? Fine. Permissiveness? Fine. License? No, for when the chips are down the teacher must be in charge. Does he guide? Does he lead? Does he direct? Select your own verb. The point is that he knows where the class is going and sees to it that it gets there.

So much for intelligence and talent. Let's look at the other element—hard work. Good classroom discipline, unless it is to be imposed by brute force, requires careful preparation by the teacher. *Not all discipline problems can be prevented, but most of them are avoided in the classrooms of intelligent, hard working teachers who plan their work effectively, who motivate their students skillfully, and who provide a friendly classroom climate.* The starting point for all preventive discipline is a good lesson, carefully prepared and skillfully executed.

The principal, in his evaluation of teaching, is guided by a mental checklist of the elements of a good lesson. Pedagogical pundits since the time of Herbart have played with a great many words in their efforts to isolate these elements. Here is our list:

1. Preparation
2. Motivation
3. Orientation
4. Presentation
5. Participation
6. Application
7. Evaluation

ESSENTIAL ELEMENTS OF AN EFFECTIVE LESSON

1. Preparation. The new teacher deposited himself heavily in a frayed armchair in the teachers' lounge. The only other person in the room was a twenty-year veteran of the algebra and geometry wars. "I envy you," the youngster sighed. The older teacher looked up from his papers. "Why?" he asked. "Oh, you don't have any preparation," was the retort. The veteran flushed and started to frame an irritable reply. Then he sighed, smiled tightly, and returned to his preparation. Perhaps a patient answer would have been more helpful, but he had heard this childlike comment once too often. No preparation indeed!

Careful planning is the foundation of all good teaching from the first day of student teaching to the last day of June of the retirement year. The nature of the lesson plan may change as the years go by, but planning should never stop.

LEARNING ABOUT THE SCHOOL SYSTEM'S CURRICULUM. Planning starts not with the daily lesson plan but with the entire school life of the student. Sooner or later most teachers will be asked to participate in curriculum planning, usually in their subject areas. Modern curriculum planning proceeds from kindergarten through high school, and sometimes beyond. Only by doing it in this way can we avoid needless repetition, overlapping, and gaps in the sequence. With all levels represented in the planning, it is possible to lay out a logical blueprint for students of all abilities in all subjects. Even if the individual teacher does not have the opportunity to serve on such a committee, his principal should see that he becomes reasonably familiar with the curriculum content of his field at each level.

Curriculum and discipline are tied closely together. A student who fails to see the relevance of what he is learning is not ready to learn. If he is not ready to learn, he may be a source of trouble. The reason he is not ready may be the illogical sequence of material which is confusing to him. While this cannot always be quickly remedied by the individual teacher, it can certainly be improved upon by the teacher who is aware of what his pupils have been exposed to in previous grades. A skillful chef can improve a mediocre stew with a few pinches of the proper herbs—providing he knows what is lacking.

THE YEAR. After at least an awareness of how the course in question fits into the total educational pattern, the teacher should plan his work for the entire year. Frequently he will have this done for him by a supervisor, but even then *he* must decide on which materials are to be stressed and which are to be skimmed over lightly. These decisions will be based on many pressures and will be particularly vexing to the teacher of courses such as American History. Before World War I, this was a one-year course in the average high school. Today it is still a one-year course in the average high school. Think of the significant material that has been added since that time! Obviously decisions must be made, and the teacher should have help in making them. Following the text is not enough. Too much material crammed into one school year in one course can cause frustration which, in turn, may lead to discipline trouble. The teacher must consider the abilities and backgrounds of his students as well as the prescribed course of study, for if he makes a fetish of covering ground he may end up covering it by himself.

THE UNIT. The next logical division of work is the unit, which may be loosely defined as any body of material requiring more than one lesson and which has a clearly discernible common theme. A unit may take three days. It may take a month. Usually it requires three or four weeks. It may be a subject unit such as World War II in history or meteorology in general science. It may be a problem unit such as intergroup relations which can be seen as a thread that runs through the entire history of man. The latter type of unit is usually chosen as a "core" around which material is presented in schools which favor the core curriculum.

Participation by students can be useful in planning approaches to the study of a unit and, sometimes, even in choosing the sequence of units. When guided by a skilled teacher, student planning does not have to lead to chaos. On the contrary, it can often be an effective insurance against irritation and boredom without the sacrifice of anything fundamental.

Units should be carefully prepared with clearly stated objectives. One should not consider this too obvious to put into words, forgetting that the students are not necessarily convinced that it is important to study *this* particular material at *this* particular time. Reliance on fear of failure or desire for good grades is simply not good enough. Learning cannot proceed effectively without motivation, and marks are rather shallow motivation. The deeper motivation that comes from a belief that there is a real need to master the unit is what you should be after, even if you cannot always get it. A good ball player may fail to hit seven times out of ten but he tries every time.

THE LESSON PLAN. The lesson plan should cover one day's work in a given subject. The first rule in preparing a lesson plan should be to err in the direction of too much material rather than too little. Too much, that is, in the *plan*, not in the actual presentation. When a teacher obviously has run out of material with ten minutes to go and resorts to a hasty device such as "Start reading the next chapter," nobody is fooled. This is the time to start throwing spitballs.

A good lesson plan is somewhat detailed but it need not be lengthy. One might well assume that a temporary indisposition would keep him home tomorrow. What plan would a substitute need to do a real good job rather than merely baby sitting? How would he like to face this lesson plan in ninth grade general science?

Mon: Cloud types, pp. 73-76
Assign pp. 77-90 Tues.

Wouldn't it be much easier to face this one?

MONDAY: *Title:* Identification of basic cloud types by appearance, altitudes, and vertical development. (Thunderheads)
Objective: To recognize and name basic cloud types in preparation for rudimentary weather forecasts.
Today's assignment: pp. 73-76, introduction to Weather unit.
Motivation: Clouds are clues to weather patterns. Recognition of clouds is fun and can be an interesting hobby. It can also help you to make rough weather forecasts from the newspaper. After you have learned to identify clouds, you will learn how forecasts are made.
Tuesday assignment: Study pp. 77-90. Memorize Table III. Bring to class in writing your identification of clouds overhead this morning just before school starts. Do not check with others so we can see who is right.
Presentation: Discuss high points of today's reading and answer questions. Explain Chart III. Run film strip, "Cloud Identification" Quiz on film strip supplement. Divide class into teams for competition.
Application: Time permitting, go outdoors for cloud identification.

2. Motivation. Salesmanship cannot be underestimated as an element in teaching. Unless the students are sold on the proposition that this course, this unit, and this lesson are important to them, little or no learning can take place. "Take my word for it, this is important," is pretty thin motivation.

A very strategic place for motivation to come out into the open is in the assignment. Here the teacher can show by advance questions, provocative statements, film strips, etc. in the "coming attractions" style, why the material is important. Here are a few basic rules for assignments:

1. Assignments must be clear. If possible, assignments should be handed out in written form, especially long term assignments. If given orally, the specific pages to be studied

should be written on the chalkboard. It would be very helpful to require students to keep assignment booklets.

2. Assignments should be given at the logical time when a look ahead is indicated. A hurried announcement made at the end of the period is not the best way to do this. To obtain maximum motivation the assignment should be given at the precise point where the students need to be shown where they are going next and why. This may be at the beginning of the period, the middle, or the end, but sufficient time should be allowed for it to be done properly.

3. Assignments should be varied according to individual abilities and needs. This calls for more work on the teacher's part, but it really does help make the course more meaningful for each student.

4. Assignments should be problem centered. They should have a clear-cut purpose tied in directly with the course. They should not be busy-work used as window dressing. Bright students quickly see through this type of assignment and either fail to do it or merely go through the motions. The result can be discipline trouble that could easily have been avoided.

5. Assignments should be of a reasonable length. There are limits to the time of even the brightest students. An exhausted adolescent is not always a model school citizen.

3. Orientation. The unfamiliar should always be related to the familiar if at all possible. Students should be shown the forest before they are asked to examine the bark of the trees. The class should be shown how each unit and each lesson proceeds from the last and meshes with the next. Even on the first day of study of a new foreign language some orientation is possible. The students can be convinced that they are not entering an uncharted wilderness by pointing out to them the similarities between the new language to be studied and their own familiar tongue.

"Yesterday we discussed the events leading to the Civil War. Today we will begin studying the War," is hardly the most effective type of orientation. A little thought would result in something much better. The point is that time should be taken consciously to consider and plan this element so that it becomes a real part of the lesson, not something that is attached as an afterthought.

4. Presentation. Teachers quickly forget that there are many ways to present facts and skills to students. The choice of methods should be based on a judgment of the best way to teach *this* material to *this* group at *this* time. Perhaps knowledge of the ability level and average span of interest of a given group may lead to a selection of two or more methods of presentation for one lesson.

The lecture method has been, and continues to be, far too popular with secondary school teachers everywhere. It can be very efficient *if* the students are listening. The trouble is that they very quickly acquire the trick of appearing to be listening. Often they can be immune to everything that is being said, especially if the lecture is a perfunctory, off-the-cuff performance. The teacher should use lectures sparingly, especially with average and below-average ability groups. Often classroom control becomes a problem simply because of excessive use of this method.

Recent research in staff utilization has renewed interest in the lecture method as an effective way of presenting some types of material to large groups. Let us note well, however, that certain ground rules attend its use:

1. The lecturer is carefully chosen and specially trained. Every good teacher is not necessarily a good lecturer. A certain amount of trial and error may precede the work of all but the most gifted large-group lecturers at the secondary school level. It is really a different kind of skill from that required in the

ordinary classroom and it usually requires careful cultivation.

2. The large-group lecturer should have sufficient extra time for the careful preparation of his material. It is not uncommon to pay the lecturer an extra stipend to work through the summer on his lectures.

Carefully prepared material, skillfully presented by an outstanding teacher can hold the interest of a very large group for a reasonable length of time. The larger the group and the lower the average intelligence of the students, the more skill is required and the shorter the lecture should be.

3. The large-group lecture should be rich with audio-visual materials to supplement the presentation of the speaker. The overhead projector is admirably suited for this purpose.

4. The large group lecture has usually been combined with small group instruction in subdivisions of 12 to 15 students and a great deal of individual project work to round out the teaching pattern. The lecture itself is rarely used, even experimentally, for more than twenty percent of the total time in a given course. In the ordinary classroom situation, lectures should be short and sweet.

The class discussion following an assigned reading is one of the most popular methods of presentation in secondary schools. This method is more effective when the class size is twenty or less, but few teachers have this advantage. If the discussion is planned carefully and led without too much domination, it can be quite effective even in a class of thirty students. Some specific techniques will be presented below.

Demonstrations can be especially useful in science classes. As a matter of fact, we note a definite trend in the teaching of such subjects as chemistry and physics away from the do-it-yourself laboratory exercises back to more efficient teacher demonstrations. It would be unfortunate to overdo this tendency since there is still great value in learning basic laboratory procedures.

Demonstration, like any other method of presentation, requires careful preparation with an accent on materials to be used. If the teacher fumbles around for equipment in the middle of a demonstration, he will not only confuse the students, but will encourage restlessness and inattention. Care should be taken so that every student can see everything that is going on. Some schools are using closed circuit T. V. for this purpose, with the camera bringing to each student the viewpoint of the instructor. Medical schools, for example, have found this very useful in demonstrating actual operations on patients to a large number of students. Some schools provide teacher's aides or lab assistants who can be useful in demonstration work. All of this costs money, of course, but some school systems seem to feel it is worth the added expense.

There are many other methods of presentation including the whole fascinating range of audio-visual aids, field trips, and guest speakers. The same basic rules are applicable for any type of presentation from lecture to field trip:

1. *Students are prepared for the experience by being told what they are about to see and hear, and why it is going to be important.*
2. *The presentation is made.*
3. *Students are reminded of what they have seen and heard and prepared for application and reinforcement of the desired learning.*

5. Participation. Students should be involved somehow in the lesson. They should do something even if it is only to answer a question now and then. Is it too elementary to devote a little space to a review of fundamental questioning techniques? Here is a suggested four step procedure for questioning during a presentation which is primarily a lecture:

1. The teacher asks the *previously prepared* question of the class as a whole. If he were to call a student's name *before* asking the question participation would cease for many of the other students.
2. After a pause during which no student is certain that lightning will not strike in his direction, he calls a student by name to answer, trying to avoid a pattern in calling on students, at least a pattern that can be detected by them. He draws out the reluctant participant as well as the one who is entranced by the sound of his own voice. Some teachers find it convenient to prepare a check sheet with students' names and space for grading by a simple code. Other teachers feel that this device hinders freedom of recitation. Each teacher should find his own answer to this problem.
3. The answer if correct, is repeated. If it is wrong, the teacher may say so in an encouraging manner, i.e., "not quite, Mary."
4. Time permitting, other students are called upon, or the teacher supplies the answer.

The foregoing procedure should be modified if a genuine discussion is being conducted. Now the questioning becomes part of the presentation rather than a semi-testing device. The responses should not be graded mechanically. As far as possible, and without calling on a student repeatedly, the teacher should encourage volunteers before calling on a student by name for an answer. In this case answers should be repeated only if the response is inaudible. At intervals the teacher, in his role as chairman, should pause for an evaluation of the direction of the entire discussion.

There are many other ways to obtain participation. Too often, teachers resort to the unimaginative method of having a handful of students writing sentences on the chalkboard while the rest of the class does nothing. There is little justification for this waste of pupil time. Pupil participation can be planned and executed so that a minimum of time is wasted. Every minute in which some or all students are doing nothing is an invitation to disciplinary problems.

6. Application. Immediate reinforcement is essential to retention in learning. Nothing succeeds like success. The skilled tennis player loves tennis. The successful learner likes his subject matter. Retention must be obtained before advancement can be made. Often retention, demonstrated by testing, is the only way to convince the student that he is succeeding. The best way to obtain this is in the immediate application of what has been learned. Proponents of teaching machines claim this as the greatest advantage of these gadgets. Be that as it may, some means of reinforcement is essential. This is rather easy in a lesson involving the application of filler to an oak board in a woodworking class. It calls for more imagination and effort when the lesson concerns the Monroe Doctrine. Filling in the blanks in a workbook (often copying them from a friend) is not the most effective application.

7. Evaluation. The presentation should be evaluated, at least by the teacher himself. The learning of the students must be evaluated. The usual methods are long or short tests with objective and subjective questions. This is not an appropriate place for a detailed treatment of this complicated topic. Suffice it to say that test and grades should be fair and clearly understood by all. The teacher would do well early in the course to reach a clear understanding with students about his philosophy of testing and marking. Nothing can contribute so quickly to poor morale as an unfair test on material which has not been adequately covered. Many students consider this a form of cheating on the part of the teacher and may themselves turn to cheating in response.

These, then, are the chief elements of a good lesson as we see it. There are other ways of listing them and there could be other elements included, but if you give each of the above items careful attention in your planning, classroom discipline should ordinarily be excellent. Special groups will require special emphases. Some of these groups will be discussed in a later chapter.

4

Special Problems of the Beginning Teacher

A common cause of failure among beginning teachers is often labelled "poor discipline." While it is convenient for the purposes of rating sheets to isolate this factor, it is hardly accurate. Some teachers lose control because they are weak in subject matter knowledge, some because they do not understand pedagogy, some because of their own poor mental health, some because of ordinary beginner's errors. The so-called "poor discipline" is really a symptom rather than a disease. It is not the point of view of this book that teachers should become engrossed in the problems of discipline per se. *They should rather concern themselves with acquiring competency in the techniques of good teaching. Good discipline will follow.* Classroom control is vital to good teaching, but it is a byproduct, not an end in itself.

HELPING THE BEGINNER

Rapidly expanding school systems have been forced to bring into the profession large numbers of beginning teachers. Principals and supervisors have found themselves devoting more and more time to the training of beginners. If we assume that they have a solid foundation in their subject fields and in the theoretical aspects of pedagogy, they still should receive some briefing in what might best be described as tricks of the trade.

We intend in this chapter to review some of these tricks. The supervisor, in introducing them to the neophytes should emphasize that none of them will work every time. On the other hand the beginner should be aware of them and should try them open-mindedly. They do represent the combined thinking of a great many successful teachers.

Emerson once said, "What you are speaks so loudly I can't hear what you say." This statement is most applicable to the classroom teacher. His voice, his manners, his appearance—everything about him has a bearing on classroom discipline. Perhaps a first consideration should be the control of his emotions, particularly anger. An angry teacher is rarely an effective teacher. He should be as impersonal as possible about misbehavior rather than regarding it as a personal affront. (It rarely is.) Emotions should be controlled by underplaying reactions to provocative situations when one is tired or not feeling well. The teacher is an educator, not an avenger.

Manners and appearance should be stressed since they are likely to set examples for many students. Seedy teachers who wear the same clothes constantly lose face in the eyes of students and contribute to the monotony which is too often part of the classroom atmosphere.

New teachers frequently have given little thought to voice training. It is neglected or ignored in most colleges and yet it is a most important tool. Beginners should be urged to tape some of their lessons and listen to the play-backs critically. The beginner frequently makes the mistake of raising his voice to compete with classroom undertones. He should be taught how to detect these noises early and to stop them at once. Almost any voice can be improved with effort. The new teacher with voice problems should have them pointed out early and frankly and encouraged to work toward improvement.

Beginning teachers, particularly young ones, are tempted to win friends by running a sort of popularity contest. A reminder is helpful that the goal should be to have students like *and* respect them. This cannot be accomplished by operating at the level of maturity of the students.

Another common failing is the tendency to become momentarily intoxicated by the presence of an uncritical and captive audience and yield to the temptation of playing the clown. Laughs are easy to obtain in the classroom and are usually no tribute to the performer's comic talent. An occasional chuckle is most desirable but the teacher should be sure that it is with him and not at him.

A warning should also be posted here about the use of sarcasm. Occasionally it can be a very sharp weapon, but like any sharp weapon it should be kept carefully sheathed and should be used only by an expert. H. L. Mencken developed it to a fine art, but if used frequently in the classroom, the user should consider himself something of a bully since the rules do not permit the students to respond in kind. It would also be a violation of common courtesy and this can become an invitation to disregard the rules of good manners in the classroom. Sarcasm can become a dangerous habit when it is used as an automatic reaction to an annoying situation.

Let us now turn to the type of specific advice that might be given to a new teacher by his principal in a series of personal conferences during his first few weeks of teaching. Obviously it cannot all be handed out at once. This would only confuse matters. Consider rather that the following constitutes a summary of a series of conferences and that the advice is being given directly to the beginner at appropriate times and in appropriate dosage.

ADVICE TO A BEGINNER

You have learned in some detail about the planning and preparation which is recommended for good teaching. This had to do mostly with the planning of the content of the course, the unit, and the lesson. In addition to this it would be helpful for you to do a bit of planning in connection with lesser matters. For one thing, you should get acquainted with the physical layout of your school, and especially your own room. You should learn where everything is kept and be ready for emergencies. You should memorize routines for fire and other emergency drills. You should know exactly how and where to obtain books and supplies.

Your seating chart with all the students' names should be ready for use. An arbitrary system such as the alphabet is most satisfactory at first. Later on, when you get to know them better, adjustments can be made to break up cliques, to seat advantageously students with visual and hearing difficulties, to keep larger students from blocking the vision of smaller ones, etc. Throughout all this preparation, try not to permit the countless details to make you nervous. If you make a mistake, or forget something, all will not be lost. Even experienced teachers occasionally drop the ball in first day confusion.

When your students arrive, get them busy immediately on the usual housekeeping chores of filling out forms, etc. Throughout this process you will be starting the important business of getting acquainted. You will have printed your name clearly on the chalkboard. Now, after a few amenities to demonstrate that you, too, are human, you might go through their names, checking on pronunciation. Another early venture should be to give a preview of your course with a strong emphasis on its importance to the students, some hints on how to study this particular material and how to use the textbook effectively, and an invitation to come for needed help after school.

Do not make the mistake of trying to do all these things in too short a span of time. Get the students involved in the work of the course as soon as you can. Much of what has been presented above sounds more time consuming than it actually is, and some of it can be saved for future meetings of the class, but do not let it be neglected too long. It should all be covered somewhere very early in the year.

Remember what we have said in the last chapter. Your students *want* to like you. The first contact is rather important so you should plan it carefully. You can show them immediately that you are pleasant and human and yet inform them that there are certain rules which you intend to enforce in your room. Your warmth and friendliness will have to cover a good deal of mileage so don't expend it all at once. Let them discover what you are like, little by little. One of the easiest rules for beginners to profess and one of the hardest for them to carry out is a rule that might be called the expanding circle of permissiveness.

Picture a small circle drawn inside a larger circle. The larger circle represents the permissive atmosphere you will eventually find workable in your classroom. The smaller circle is where you should try to start. It is natural and easy to work out from a stricter atmosphere to a good, workable relationship. If you try to reverse the direction of the arrows and start with an easy atmosphere, you will find it difficult to work back to a smaller circle. It is a bit like the difference between climbing a mountain and returning down the slope. Mountain climbing may be challenging, but why try it in your classroom?

A common cause of disciplinary trouble is the collision between teacher-student backgrounds. When this happens to you, you should be very patient and bear in mind that ability

and talent may be hiding anywhere, even under a dirty face! Yours is now the responsibility to discover this ability, to encourage it, and to develop this ability, to the optimum, not because the world needs it—but simply because it exists. Even without ability or talent, each child is a human being and a young American and has been promised equality of opportunity. He may ultimately reject your standards. You should not regard this as failure or as a personal affront. You are in no position to say that your values are always the best for all people.

Tolerance is a thin word for what we are trying to get across here. You will be a more effective teacher if your actions speak acceptance rather than mere tolerance. This does not mean that you accept their standards for yourself, but rather that you accept their right to hold them. Then it becomes easier for you to try to raise their sights to values which you feel are more desirable. When you assume the role of a teacher you undertake to teach *all* children, not merely those with clean shirts, quick minds, or good manners.

Your efforts to learn about your students should take on two aspects: first to learn about them as individuals because this is most important; and then to assess them as groups, for you will find that each one of your classes has a personality of its own. Individual information can be found in the guidance files. Be very careful about the interpretation of this data. Individual test scores can be misleading by themselves if taken out of context. Don't be afraid to ask questions of experienced guidance personnel. They are there to help you.

A good way to win the loyalty of your students is to show them that you are truly concerned about them, individually and as groups. Demonstrate, for example, your interest in the non-academic life of the school by some attendance at the athletic events, plays, and dances. Share their elation over an important athletic victory and let them know that you know the standing of the teams. This takes very little time and can pay rich dividends. The important thing is not to pretend that you are interested in these things. *Get* interested in them.

When it becomes necessary to reprimand an individual, be conscious of the general prudential rules: *reprimand in private, praise in public.* Punishment will be discussed in some detail in a later chapter, but at this point we must mention the importance to you of clearly understood justice. Adolescents have a very keen sense of right and wrong and are extremely sensitive to fairness on the part of teachers. The beginning teacher will find it expedient to be very careful in doling out punishment. If it is fair, it will be readily accepted. If it is unfair, the group will rally to the cause of a martyr. As time goes by and you establish yourself, an error like this will most likely be overlooked. At the beginning, however, a tactical error in meting out justice may lead to the hasty conclusion that you are an unfair person. This is difficult to live down.

Try to avoid statements beginning, "When I was your age. . . ." This almost invariably destroys communication with adolescents because they have heard it so often that they are weary of it.

Another practice that is very distasteful to adolescents is being compared to other students or, especially, to their own brothers or sisters. The beginning teacher is usually in no position to make this comparison because she does not know the older siblings, but it is sometimes thoughtlessly done by experienced teachers. We can understand, perhaps, parents making this tactical error since they have usually not had training or experience in these matters. It is inexcusable for a teacher.

YOUR CLASSROOM ATMOSPHERE

Within your room you will find the option to exercise many choices. Modern supervision is not keyed to telling you how to do everything, but rather to offering you help (when you need it) in doing the things *you* decide to do. Here and there in our secondary schools there still lingers the tyrannical principal or supervisor, but he is becoming rather rare.

Your supervisors will be anxious to observe you and to help you after you have your feet on the ground. They want you to get started right and they are extremely anxious to find out if you are going to make good. Once they have confidence in you they will very likely leave you alone. You may, indeed, find yourself asking them to visit you. This will not mean that they have lost interest in you. It usually reflects the lack of time given to supervisors to do their supervising.

The creation of classroom atmosphere is your problem. The physical conditions attendant to this will be discussed in a later chapter for we consider them most important. Let us assume for the moment that your room is in good physical condition. Now you are ready to create the kind of intellectual atmosphere that is conducive to learning.

Perhaps it might be useful to illustrate what we mean by describing briefly some *bad* examples of classroom atmosphere. Here are three samples which we hope will not be familiar to you:

1. The Gestapo atmosphere. Heavy restraint is very much evident and is imposed by a strong personality. The teacher seems to be constantly sitting on a lid he has placed on a miniature volcano. Punishment, group and individual, lingers heavily in the air. When the teacher turns his back and someone snickers, everyone is assigned five more homework problems. There is a faint chorus of groans. Five more problems are assigned. Now there is a sullen silence. To the untrained observer, discipline might seem to be very good, but what would happen if the teacher were to leave the room? What is erroneously thought of as military discipline seems effective as long as supervision is strict and constant, but when restraints are removed it often falls apart. Actually, good military discipline is nothing like this.

A democratic atmosphere, contrary to what the Gestapo teacher may think, does not have to be chaotic or disruptive. It is simply the positive counterpart of what has been described above. Restraint comes largely from within the pupils and is accepted because interesting things are happening in the classroom. Each student is respected as an individual and the teacher commands a special respect because he is the key to the learning process and his firm, guiding hand is quietly present everywhere.

2. The soap opera atmosphere. The teacher, having difficulty in maintaining order, resorts to various types of emotional blackmail. She appeals to the class to pity her real or fancied ailments. She bemoans the way they are repaying her for the love she has lavished on them. This is a particularly nauseating manifestation but it does happen now and then.

A teacher with a healthy mental attitude seldom is trapped into emotional reactions. On the contrary, she acts as an emotional balance wheel which minimizes disturbances caused by emotionally upset pupils.

3. The dog-eat-dog atmosphere. Here the teacher places a heavy emphasis on competition, posting class standings for all to see. Students are frequently reprimanded for poor work. "I'm ashamed of the work you did on the last test!" he says to the whole class. Perhaps what he ought to be saying is "I'm ashamed of the teaching I evidently did in preparation for this test." The teacher imitates the manner of a temperamental conductor at a bad symphony rehearsal. This sometimes seems to get results but emotions like these are hard to sustain. Where does the teacher go from here?

Competition is an acknowledged stimulus to learning if used in moderation and under realistic conditions (where the competitors are really able to compete on equal terms). Co-operation is also an important classroom stimulant which wears much better and longer than overemphasized competitive zeal.

The most positive approach to a good classroom atmosphere can be through the use of *esprit de corps*. Everyone likes to be part of a going concern. Subtle appeals to school spirit, class spirit, or homework spirit, can be very successful in building a good atmosphere.

The teacher need never tolerate impertinence or poor manners to avoid a poor atmosphere. The trick is entirely in how he handles himself. A classroom is a place to work. Work can, and should, be enjoyable. It's all up to you.

As a new teacher, you will discover that certain problems are common to most schools and are no reflection on your ability. You should be prepared for them and will usually be able to avoid trouble by some elementary precautions.

One of these perennial headaches, which has been mentioned in the last chapter, is cheating on tests and quizzes. It would be helpful if you made your position clear at the very beginning. A set of specific ground rules should be laid down. Here is a sample set of rules which some teachers have found very useful.

1. No books or papers are to be permitted on the desks or on the floor adjacent to the desks. (Tell them where to put these materials on test days.)

2. There will be absolutely no communication with anyone except the teacher during a test. A raised hand will bring the teacher to the student.

3. If a student *seems* to be looking at another student's paper, the assumption will be that he is cheating. (Actually this is strongly stated, but it has been found to be most effec-

tive. The teacher will, in fact, exercise careful judgment in his observation.)

4. There will be no turning from a face-front position.

5. There will be no trips anywhere during the test. (During longer tests this may be relaxed to take care of normal needs.)

6. Any violation of these rules will result in the student's paper being quietly confiscated. An appeal may be made privately after school. There will be no lengthy discussion unless the teacher is clearly in error.

Sound familiar? It should. That does not make it less effective. It sounds familiar because it works. The important points to remember are that these rules are clearly and forcefully explained *before* any testing takes place and that confiscation and appeal are private matter between teacher and student. All evidences of cheating should be turned over to the principal or the proper disciplinary officer. It is not essential that that official should punish the guilty party. That can be your job, and a zero for the test is usually enough punishment. The administration should know about it, however, because it may be an important link in the understanding of an individual student.

Seasonal and diurnal letdowns are often perplexing to the new teacher. The diurnal letdowns, usually evident before lunch or before the close of school, can be countered by a change of pace in the presentation or a brief seventh inning stretch during which the students are asked to stand up and perhaps to converse briefly among themselves. At the same time the windows could be opened for a moment even on a cold day. This whole process could take place in a minute or less and might be worth it in increased efficiency for the rest of the period.

The seasonal letdown is a bit more difficult to deal with. This phenomenon occurs just before holidays and just after examination periods. It is important to hold the line in good spirits and with an extra amount of tolerance. Most schools have found it useful to establish rules for these days in order to promote some consistency. A teacher cannot hold the fort alone.

There is no question about it, Mr. Beginning Teacher, you have your work cut out for you. Teaching in the secondary schools is hardly a soft touch. Would you have chosen this career if it were? We hope not. You will be expected to carry your share of the load, especially in discipline. The administration is there to help you when you need help, but you will be expected to handle routine problems yourself. How you go about it is pretty much up to you—but we think these suggestions will help.

5

Special Handling: The Physically Handicapped

An effective teacher soon learns that there is no simple set of rules which always applies to every case in school discipline. He learns to operate from a working philosophy rather than from rule of thumb. On the other hand, it is most desirable to understand certain rules and then attempt to apply them in appropriate situations. This is particularly true in dealing with special types of youngsters. Among these would be the physically handicapped.

Since it would be impractical in this volume to deal with the special problems of each specific type of handicap, we shall limit ourselves to suggestions which might be helpful to the teacher in working with students who have any type of serious physical handicap. Estimates vary widely as to the number of children in American schools at a given time who are handicapped physically, but two facts seem clear:

1. Teachers have always had to work with a small percentage of physically handicapped youngsters. Often the teachers are not aware of the fact that they are handicapped.

When this fact was pointed out by one of the authors in a graduate course for teachers, he was challenged by one of his students who thought it was a waste of time to discuss these problems since they involved so few youngsters. A week later the same student admitted that inquiries at his school revealed many handicapped students enrolled.

"I even give one of them a ride to school every morning," he said, "and I didn't even know he wore an artificial leg. I wondered why he wasn't out for basketball. I'm glad now I didn't ask him."

2. The number of handicapped youngsters in our schools will undoubtedly increase in the future because of a shift in policy away from the segregation of this population. Many specialists feel that even severely handicapped students, once they have been trained in the special skills required by their conditions, should be placed with normal children as much as possible.

Our society has accepted the principle that the handicapped should be cared for and given every opportunity for happiness and usefulness. This imposes on us a responsibility which will be discharged only when every handicapped member of our society has been given all possible opportunities for adjustment. One can readily see that this is quite a challenge for all of us. It cuts across the fields of many specialists and volunteers. Perhaps the most important of these, next to the parents, are the teachers.

General guidelines. The teacher will soon discover that the special handling involved in working with handicapped youngsters sometimes amounts to a studied *avoidance* of special handling. The best generalization to begin with might be that these youngsters are, except for their handicaps, *like normal children only more so.* Their personal needs are underscored by their handicaps. They need security, a sense of belonging, and (especially) experiences in truly successful accomplishment. Standards should *not* be lowered for them unless their particular handicaps make certain tasks obviously impossible. Their punishment should be like that given to other children. Their rewards should be like those given to other children.

One teacher in a private school experienced great difficulties in dealing with a seventh grade boy whose slightly defective heart did not permit him normal outlets in play. He had been handled with extreme permissiveness by his parents and by his teachers all through his early years and he took advantage of the situation by extremely rude behavior. After trying everything else, the teacher in desperation resorted to a private session in which she reprimanded him severely and warned him that future misbehavior would result in immediate punishment. (The nature of which was not defined.)

After the initial shock, the boy responded very well. Subsequent lapses into misconduct almost took on the nature of test cases to see if the teacher meant business. Reprimands almost seemed to please him. No punishment was necessary, happily. At last he was being treated like an ordinary boy—something that nobody had tried before!

The emotional adjustment problems of handicapped students are somewhat greater and more specialized than those of normal students, but maladjustments in the case of the former are not universal. The degree of maladjustment depends on such factors as: degree and effect on appearance of the handicap; changing degree of handicap (improvement); intelligence of the student; and attitudes of parents, teachers, and friends.

It should be remembered that the great goal beyond adjustment is the preparation of the handicapped to become *self-dependent,* useful members of society. A teacher cannot always make direct contributions to this goal, but conscious efforts to help the student see the relationship between the classwork he is doing and a realistic occupational goal may help a great deal.

Special needs of handicapped students. The teacher can deal more successfully with the handicapped youngsters if he understands their special needs. Although the teacher, alone, cannot meet or even contribute to the meeting of some of these needs, he prepares himself to become an effective member of a team that will attempt the task. The following list has been developed out of an extensive reading in the area. Since so much of the literature is repetitive it would be extremely difficult to cite specific sources.

Physical needs:

1. Special therapeutic exercises for the afflicted parts.
2. Healthful exercise for the whole body or compensatory and substitutive activity.
3. Expressive and emotional outlets in normal play and games.

Intellectual needs:

1. Intensive vocational guidance with an emphasis on the adjustment of overly high goals or too modest goals.
2. Early and intensive training in vocational skills.
3. Scholastic achievement standards as normal as possible.

Personality needs:

1. Consistent, wholesome parental, teacher, and peer attitudes, avoiding:
   a. Rejection
   b. Overprotection
   c. Pressing compensatory intellectual achievements beyond abilities.
2. Specialized guidance to overcome:
   a. Withdrawing, reticent, asocial behavior.
   b. Refusal to recognize real conditions; concealment, delusions.

c. Feelings of inferiority.
d. Extremely aggressive, competitive behavior.
e. Anxiety, tension, nervousness, temper tantrums.

3. Carefully moderated affection, praise, and attention.
4. Avoidance of attention to injury motivated by pity. (Normal and casual acceptance of injury is a desirable goal.)
5. Examples of successful people who have overcome handicaps. (Theodore Roosevelt, Franklin Roosevelt, Helen Keller, etc.)
6. Realistic success and accomplishment.

Social needs:

1. Opportunities to achieve social acceptance.
2. Guidance in achieving some degree of independence.
3. Opportunities of constructive, useful work.

Specific recommendations for teachers. Most teachers react sympathetically to handicapped students. This sympathy should be tempered with a knowledge of the special needs of the student, and should not be permitted to become obvious in teacher-student relationships. The time of the teacher is limited. He should use judgment in dealing with any individual so that he does not neglect the group. On the other hand, he cannot approach his job solely as a group manipulator. Each student is entitled to *some* individual attention. The handicapped student does not necessarily require more individual attention than the normal student, but it should be *a different kind of attention.* Here are some suggestions addressed directly to the teacher who has one or more handicapped students in his classes:

1. You should learn the common symptoms of maladjustment and try to apply appropriate guidance and teaching techniques. Most of these symptoms could be observed in

non-handicapped students, but the chances are far greater of seeing them in the handicapped.

A firm, friendly hand is needed in guiding these youngsters toward *reality*. The maladjustments are usually the direct result of conditions associated with the handicap and are not necessarily deeply rooted. Potentially the handicapped child is a normal person whose equilibrium has been temporarily upset. He usually responds very nicely to a healthy atmosphere. If not, you should make an effort to enlist the cooperation of the parents. Failing in this, a referral should be made to an agency. It is usually easy to obtain this help if you simply know where to turn for it.

2. You can apply realistic scholastic standards. This has been mentioned above but it bears repetition. There is a strong tendency on that part of all of us to overprotect the handicapped child. This is most evident in marks given for classroom work. The line of reasoning seems to be that since the student's opportunities to achieve have been limited, he must be *given* success in academic work because of its non-physical nature. The trouble is that this encourages overly ambitious goals. Bitter disappointment may follow. The child may wear braces on his legs, but his feet should be firmly planted on the ground. It can be cruelly unfair to lead him to believe that he has abilities which he does not have. It is far wiser to develop and exploit the abilities which he does have.

If, for example, a crippled child shows a modest but real talent for art, it is possible that he can utilize this talent to greater accomplishment than a normal child could even with greater talent. The handicap might, in fact, become an advantage since the student is forced into longer periods of sedentary activity than his normal friends. The teacher who can help him to utilize these long hours to advantage is performing a real service.

3. You can try to cooperate closely with parents. The rea-

sons are obvious and mainly associated with the creation of a healthy and consistent atmosphere for adjustment. There are other reasons too. You need, for example, to understand what the parents consider sufficient reasons for tardiness and absence, etc. You need to know what physical requirements are being prescribed at the moment. If the physician recommends an increase in exercise, you should become aware of this and would not then allow the student to remain in at recess. A handicapped child is just as likely to have lazy days as a normal child.

4. You can cooperate with agencies. The school nurse or physician may be consulted as to which agencies are involved. As a matter of good practice, the administration would ordinarily supply this information to you before you get the student.

5. You can work to correct improper attitudes on the part of normal children. Maladjustment in non-handicapped students may well show up in their attitudes toward the handicapped. This is more commonly demonstrated in attitudes toward mental than physical handicaps, but it does appear from time to time as a reaction to any type of abnormality in a new student. It is essential for the welfare of all that these poor attitudes be discovered and corrected. As a matter of fact, one of the arguments advanced by those who wish to integrate handicapped youngsters with normal groups is that their presence there will be a healthy thing *for the non-handicapped.* The development of a sensible attitude toward handicapped people is a normal part of anyone's education.

6. You can help the handicapped student in finding a realistic occupational goal or a related set of goals to choose from. This is not normally a responsibility of the classroom teacher, and you should be careful not to hand out advice or opinions too heavily. Your approach might well be to assist the student in finding his own answers. It might also be helpful for you

to brush up on some of the literature on non-directive counseling techniques in preparation for this task since this type of counseling has been found quite effective in dealing with handicapped youngsters.

Thus you will find yourself in a strategic position to help handicapped students in their adjustments to various problems and in their search for a productive and useful life. Because of the small numbers of students involved and because of the relative intensity of their problems, you might lean a little more in the direction of guidance and might work a little harder to correlate your efforts with the other teachers involved than you ordinarily could. You do not have to become a specialist, but you can learn a good deal from the specialists. As is true in any type of good teaching, intelligence, imagination, understanding, and hard work will go a long way.

6

Special Handling: Slow and Rapid Learners

One of the most frequently cited sources of discipline trouble in the secondary school is the slow learner. Depending upon the school and its program, his I.Q. will range from 80 downward. His difficulties may stem from a variety of causes, but he is almost always a slow reader. His comprehension of abstract material is very slow and he finds it difficult to apply any given principle to a new situation. He does not do very well the kinds of things that are usually done in the classroom. By the time he has reached the seventh grade he has been subjected to years of frustration—both at home and at school.

He discovered very early in life that people considered him different somehow. As a result of this he is sometimes more sensitive than other students. To make matters worse, the things he has trouble with are the things adults seem to consider most important, although he cannot understand why. At home he may have been pitied or rejected (or both, in alternating doses), and in any case he has been made fully aware of his family's disappointment in him.

One teacher recalls a poignant incident in which she discovered one of her duller 16-year-old students sitting in a field with his arm around a collie dog early one spring evening.

"Hi, Charlie," she greeted him. "How come you're not home having dinner?"

"I'll eat when they're through," was the reply. "I'd rather sit here with Prince. He doesn't think I'm so dumb."

If the slow learner is normal in other respects he can be expected to react against this frustrating situation sooner or later. Sometimes this reaction will take the form of anti-social behavior of an open and overt nature. Sometimes it may consist of slipping quietly into the lavatory to record his emotions on the walls in angry words. Unless his teachers and parents can convince him that he can find a useful and dignified place in society, he may enlist in the army of delinquency and crime, or drift into a parasitic existence.

In our society it is expensive to be poor. The poor buy many things on the installment plan, thereby paying the full list price plus a healthy interest rate. This adds to the misery of poverty by an unwise use of the meager purchasing power the poor do have. So it is with the slow learner in the average school system. He does not have much I. Q. to "spend" and much of what he does have is wasted. Because he cannot respond effectively to ordinary classroom procedures he often is sent on errands for the teacher to keep him out of the way. He claps blackboard erasers together outside the building and carries the wastebaskets to the incinerator while his classmates are learning. Ironically, he may learn more from the custodian than he does from his teachers. This makes him happy for the moment since he is relieved of the immediate heartaches of the classroom. It relieves the teacher momentarily of a perplexing problem. This is just as effective as sweeping dirt under the rug. Now, instead of learning very little, he learns next to nothing. The problem is postponed but it continues to grow like a snowball rolling down a hill of sticky snow.

By the time the slow learner reaches junior high school he has usually resigned himself to leaving school at the earliest legal time—often on the morning of his sixteenth birthday. This compounds the problems of the junior high school, especially in terms of discipline. Now the student is frankly marking time and makes no effort to use what little intelligence he does have. Even a junior high school with a sound program for slow learners has great difficulty in persuading many of these students to remain in school and to work up to their capacities. The twig has been badly bent.

When the few survivors finally get to high school, the situation becomes even worse. The rate of attrition itself often precludes the possibility of grouping slow learners together without running into prohibitive instructional costs. Only the large high schools can do this effectively under the usual conditions. Thus the slow learner who reaches high school finds himself grouped with average, and sometimes bright students in academic classes. Another problem now presents itself as a question of policy when the school system does succeed in preventing him from dropping out along the way. If the slow learner attends high school long enough, does his very best in every way, and is a good citizen, is he entitled to a regular diploma? Are there arbitrary achievement standards for a diploma? What are they? What about a "certificate of attendance" as a sort of bargain basement diploma? These are red hot issues in the high school which manages, by virtue of an effective program, to retain the slow learners. Opinions are varied and very strong.

It is not the opinion of the authors that policy should be imposed on a reluctant faculty in this matter. For many decades we have tried to implement the policy of education for *all* American youth. This has resulted in a wide variety of program offerings at the high school level. The diploma, itself, has lost its meaning as an arbitrary and uniform badge of achievement. Now employers and colleges turn to more meaningful data such as transcripts, class standings, test results, recommendations, etc. for an appraisal of the individual student. This does not mean that we have abandoned standards of achievement. It merely means that we have rejected the policy of "train the best and shoot the rest." If the issue of a diploma becomes a red herring that obscures the trail of a meaningful program for slow learners, why fight the issue? The program is the important thing! Far better to have a slow learner graduate with a "certificate of attendance" than to have him lose the benefits of two or three years of education over a technicality.

We should seek especially answers to the educational problems of students with an I. Q. range of 70 to 89 in our secondary schools. (A strong case could even be made for dropping the lower end of this arbitrary limit to 50.) Students brighter than this find their opportunities in the regular school situation. Students slower than this usually find help in more specialized institutions or in the world of work. Perhaps this policy may emulate that of dealing with physically handicapped students someday, in which case the comprehensive high school would become comprehensive indeed. For the present, however, we must recognize the fact that we are not equipped for this work.

One high school went to a good deal of trouble to isolate a group of 15 very slow learners in the tenth grade and to assign them to sympathetic and superior teachers. A series of conferences preceded the assignments in which the teachers were briefed by "experts," but the experiment failed to produce anything more than friendly baby sitting as the year progressed. The teachers had neither the training, the experience, nor the special facilities to deal with this group which was unusually low in intelligence. Good intentions and a sprinkling of advice are simply not enough.

What is the slow learner like? Sometimes the *very* slow learner fits the Hollywood image of the village idiot. Stone-faced and uncomprehending, he misses most of what goes on around him and can communicate only haltingly. More often this is not true at all. The average slow learner looks like any other student. He is carefree and gay and quite often assumes the role of the class clown. There are several reasons for this. It is a wonderful compensation for dullness. Here is a way to attract attention—to amount to something. Doesn't everyone love a clown? Then there is the matter of understanding responsibility. Slow learners can relax easier than bright students simply because they do not understand the complexities of life and its sometimes terrifying responsibilities. Theirs is a child-like existence which rarely leads to ulcers.

The difference between the slow learner and his normal peers comes into sharp focus when he is asked to read and when he is asked to string together facts and to generalize from them. He finds great difficulty in even remembering facts unless he is highly motivated. The motivation can be crude but it must be real to him. He can be taught attitudes, but not indirectly by a presentation of facts. The teaching must be direct and repetitive and quickly reinforced by applications. Transfer of training from one learning situation to another is nearly hopeless. He does not understand that attention seeking by misbehavior in class is wrong because it interferes with the learning opportunities of other students. He learns to cooperate because misbehavior brings unhappiness and punishment.

What does the slow learner need? Many of the needs of the slow learner are similar in kind, if not in degree, to the needs of all youngsters his age. On the other hand, he has some special needs which the teacher should be aware of. Some of these are:

1. Individual professional evaluation. An attempt should be made at an early age to determine the reason for his condition. Frequently cases are cited in which an alleged slow learner turns out to be simply a child who cannot see or hear well. Such neglect is unnecessary today. Often a brain injury or a psychological block causes the bottleneck to learning. Special treatment would then be required. Slow learners should be carefully tested *individually* and with appropriate tests to determine accurately their aptitudes and achievements. Mass testing has a tendency to make them look worse than they are. The teacher needs to know exactly what she is dealing with.

2. A meaningful and appropriate curriculum. Ancient history is a very questionable morsel for a child who has difficulty in understanding the relationship between yesterday and last week. The slow learner's curriculum should be practical but not merely utilitarian. Shops and home economics suites are not always the answers. Appropriate material should be selected from the usual fields of social studies, English, mathematics, and science, as well as from the non-academic areas. The slow learner is going to live in the same society as the rapid learner. His vote will actually be *more* important since he has the rapid learner vastly outnumbered.

3. Appropriate remedial instruction, particularly in reading. His reading ability may be limited but he should be brought up as closely as possible to that limit. This remedial instruction should not be of the usual academic type, but suited to his needs as well as to his known limitations.

4. Success at some academic tasks. Like any other youth, he needs success. Unlike other youths, he has had very little. A 100 percent quiz paper on material geared to his level means so very much to him once in a while! On the other hand, he must maintain a realistic idea of his own limitations. Striking this delicate balance is one of the stimulating challenges of teaching.

5. FIRMNESS AND CONSISTENCY. The teacher must never surrender in the struggle to keep the slow learner working up to his capacity. Sometimes he must be driven hard. He never should be permitted to feel that the teacher doesn't care. Discipline should also be keyed to firmness and consistency, tempered with understanding.

6. PATIENCE. The slow learner responds best to a mature, well-balanced teacher who likes her work and has a tremendous amount of patience and understanding. Sometimes beginners take instinctively to this work, but more often it calls for an experienced teacher. In any event, no teacher should be drafted into the work or tempted into it merely by extra pay. This is a highly specialized task which should be looked upon as a professional challenge of the highest order.

How to teach slow learners. The first question is one of grouping. Some argue for homogeneous grouping of slow learners in all subjects. Others feel that these youngsters can profit most by being integrated with normal students. Perhaps an answer lies in compromise. When there are enough "survivors" they can be grouped in academic subjects. The groups should be small, no larger than twenty. In non-academic subjects they could be put into regular groups. Life is like that. On their jobs they will probably work with others like themselves. At the polls, in the barber shops, and at the ball game they will rub elbows with everyone. The teacher does not usually choose the manner of grouping, and must work with slow learners either in an integrated or a segregated class. Let us consider both.

When the slow learner is part of a "normal" class it means more work for the teacher. He must find special materials for him to supplement the text or to substitute for the text. He must give him extra help or arrange for someone else to give him help. Sometimes a bright student can be found to volunteer for this duty. In this case, the volunteer tutor should have some instruction from the teacher so that he does not simply do the work for the slow student. This can become a very profitable relationship for both students if properly supervised. One gets the needed help and the other experiences the real satisfaction of service.

Frequent conferences will be helpful to reinforce what learning does take place and to keep the whole process moving, as well as to supply injections of encouragement. During class periods the teacher could also try to encourage participation by the slow learner regularly so that he does not feel left out. Simple oral questions which he can answer publicly will do a world of good. Special projects such as charts, maps, or models can sometimes be assigned within the limits of his abilities. The ideal device, of course, is the project requiring a special skill in which he surpasses his classmates. A model blockhouse constructed by a nimble-fingered slow learner and exhibited in a social studies classroom can provide a very special magic.

Grouped slow learners are something else again and are commonly assigned to a beginning teacher in a perverted application of seniority rights in the mediocre school. Now the problem of suitable materials becomes paramount. The slow learner responds very nicely to appropriate audio-visual aids if he has been prepared for what he is to see and hear and if the material to be retained is hammered home by the teacher after the presentation. Materials that outrage the student's sense of maturity should be avoided. Reading material simple in vocabulary yet aimed at an older interest level, has become increasingly available lately. It is folly to ask a teenager to read about the "Easter Bunny" simply because he is a poor reader. Abridged editions of the same literature being read by normal groups are ideal since this softens the emphasis on his academic handicaps. We cannot hide his weakness from the slow learner or from his friends, but there is no point in needlessly rubbing his nose in it.

Distractions in the classroom should be carefully minimized. Chalkboards should be clean unless in use and any other potential attention getters should be eliminated if possible. It is even a good idea to have cloth covers to throw over models or displays when they are not in use. This would be a sound practice for a classroom serving any type of students, but it is particularly important in the case of slow learners because of their short span of interest.

Informality is often successful in working with slow learners but it must be used with caution. It is most important for these youngsters to enjoy their classes. The chances are that school has been a pretty grim business for them. On the other hand, they have a tendency to overplay any comedy that creeps into the classroom. The teacher must maintain firm control at these times, but it is far easier to go along with a reasonable amount of fun than to try to stamp it out. Like Communism, it thrives underground.

Firmness is also essential in dealing with the continuous nuisance of "forgotten" books and pencils. This is often petty sabotage aimed at delaying the disagreeable business of learning. There should be a penalty that annoys the annoyer. Retaining the forgetful ones after school usually does the trick, but a little imagination on your part can provide penalties that more nearly fit the crime.

Frequent changes of pace are necessary, for their span of interest is short. The same material can be presented by a variety of techniques during one class period. Twenty minutes is a reasonable limit for any one type of presentation, certainly for anything resembling a lecture.

The teacher should never mix discipline with academic penalties, especially in dealing with slow learners. These people have enough trouble with grades without adding further misery to the situation. On the contrary, one should look for ways to reward extra effort with extra credit to open up avenues of hope. Motivation must be direct and easy to understand. Slow learners have found little joy in learning and must be taught that it does exist.

Routine is very important for the slow learner since it gives him a feeling of security. He likes repetitive, simple tasks that would drive a brighter student wild. Industry recognizes this and prefers to hire the slow learner for certain tasks on the assembly line. The teacher can profit from the experience of industry by breaking his lessons down into small, repetitive steps, and by employing easy exercises for reinforcement soon after the presentation.

Above all, when a teacher is assigned to slow learners as part of his task or as his entire task, he should be reminded that he is not only attempting a job which most teachers detest, he is also doing work which most teachers simply cannot do. The hope of our nation lies not only in the development of leaders but also in the development of followers. A teacher who has helped to guide the multitude of slow learners into productive citizenship and away from the relief rolls or prisons has accomplished a real service to society.

RAPID LEARNERS

The teaching of gifted students also involves special problems. These students are quickly recognized by their eager curiosity and creative imaginations. They read rapidly and with easy comprehension. They enjoy learning and tax the skill of the teacher. Surprisingly enough to some, disciplinary problems of the first magnitude can rise out of these groups. These problems are nearly always rooted in poor teaching. Such students have a low tolerance for repetition, poor quality homework assignments based on more of the same, and a general lack of challenge in the lesson. Bright students resent being segregated merely to give them more work.

There are many popular misconceptions about bright youngsters that can be extremely misleading. First, there is the "egg-head" notion that characterizes them as being weak, sickly, near sighted, and eccentric. A few of them may be, but most of them are quite the opposite. Bright youngsters are usually superior in many different ways, including athletic skills. They are frequently popular. It is often true that they prefer associations with older persons, but they also value the acceptance of their age-mates. As a matter of fact they sometimes work deliberately below capacity (especially the girls) in order to conform to the standards of their age group. The more sophisticated ones learn to underplay their abilities in order to gain greater acceptance.

Bright students have wide interests and often exhibit tendencies to spread themselves too thinly over many activities. They quickly sense the scarcity of superior intelligence in their society and become sorely tempted to run things everywhere. They frequently exhibit a good sense of humor but sometimes have a tendency toward sarcasm when frustrated by the slow thinking of their peers or their teachers.

Their emotional reactions are frequently accentuated by their intelligence with fairly rapid shifts in mood from hilarity to sullen silence or depression. When too much pressure is applied, tears may result. They are more like spirited race horses than stolid workhorses.

Special needs of rapid learners.

1. A CHALLENGING CURRICULUM. They need a pace suited to their nimble minds, a pace that eliminates boredom and stimulates imaginative thinking. At the same time, boredom must not be eliminated by sugar coating or the exclusion of essential materials. Lightweight courses are very boring to

these people. Conventional blocks of material covering one year such as Algebra I, French I, etc. must be re-examined and made more flexible. One year's work for a given group may take half a year or three quarters of a year. Perhaps the basic content of a year's work may be retained but enriched with stimulating applications and illustrations. These are administrative questions which must be settled with participation from all levels from kindergarten through graduate school. A good starting point might be an agreement on definition of such currently popular terms as *ability grouping, acceleration,* and *enrichment.* Everyone in education is using these terms today. We ought to agree on exactly what we mean in this application of the terms.

2. CONTINUED ENCOURAGEMENT AND REWARD FOR QUALITY ACHIEVEMENT. If we group rapid learners, raise the standards of achievement for the group and then reward them with a "C" because they are being measured by a different yardstick, we will soon find the numbers in these groups dwindling. This treatment outrages their sense of justice.

"I would have had an A in a regular division!" they protest. "Now I won't get into a good college." We counter, "Yes, but you are in an honors division. This is indicated by an asterisk on your record and the colleges are more interested in that than the C." Then they look at us with the frankly skeptical look usually reserved for used-car salesmen.

3. GUIDANCE TO MINIMIZE CONCEIT. The current emphasis on intellectual achievement has put us in a position where bright youngsters are tempted to overestimate their abilities. They have heard too often about their high I.Q.'s and in their immaturity have assumed an air of superiority. This is not a serious situation and can usually be corrected by guidance. It should not be ignored.

4. GUIDANCE IN LEARNING TO ACCEPT AND RESPECT UNINTELLIGENT PEOPLE. Rapid learners must learn that they constitute a

small minority in our society and that the majority has rights. They must be taught that persons with low verbal aptitudes often have many superior qualities and skills that are worthy of sincere respect and admiration.

5. Opportunities to develop their non-academic skills. Bright students need to learn all of the skills essential to good living just as any students do. They need strong and healthy bodies. They need to learn to use their hands and to appreciate the arts. Current pressures and antiquated schedules sometimes make this very difficult for them.

How to teach rapid learners. When the teacher has a bright student in an average class, he faces special problems just as he does with the dull youngster in the same class. He must work that much harder in providing materials appropriate for his level of achievement. The superior youngster's assignments must be individualized for best results. This does not mean that the teacher should assign him twenty problems for homework when the rest of the class has ten. He may need only five and he should be permitted to contribute to the class without dominating the scene. More time for individual conferences should be provided without neglecting the rest of the group. The same argument prevails here as the one over segregating the slow learners. The same common-sense solution is available. When a school has enough genuinely rapid learners at a given level, it should try to group them in the subjects in which they excel. A rapid learner in English may be very ordinary in Chemistry. While it is quite true that there are sharp differences even among students in so-called homogeneous groups, the differences are not quite as pronounced as they are in a random group. Most teachers feel that better work can be accomplished when rapid learners are grouped together.

In working with bright groups a teacher will find that a

routine teaching performance, using stereotyped methods, is just not good enough. A class period should not be wasted in simply repeating facts that have been read. Assignments should be imaginative and stimulating. The text should be supplemented with original source material. The teacher must be aware of individual differences and interests and do something about them in making work assignments. Long range, larger units of work involving original research can be assigned. Essay questions should outnumber objective types on tests and quizzes. *Note well, however, that the amount of outside work required of these students should be reasonable.* The magic is in quality rather than in mere quantity. They are usually very active in school affairs, including sports, and are normally carrying five academic subjects. If every teacher feels duty-bound to load rapid learners with ever-increasing amounts of work, the net result is often frustration, failure, and discipline trouble.

Many school systems group gifted students for acceleration (covering material faster) and enrichment (digging deeper). These programs are becoming particularly popular in secondary schools. An example of one such program in grades 7-12 may be rapidly reviewed in the following excerpts from a descriptive brochure developed by one of the writers for presentation to college admissions officers with the transcripts of participants. This brochure describes, in general, the enrichment program (thus far the terms *enrichment* and *acceleration* have been used interchangeably in this system) in the four secondary schools of Cranston, Rhode Island, and is used by the Guidance Department of Cranston High School East.

> . . . The program was planned to challenge the more gifted and/or highly motivated students to move more rapidly and in greater depth through the various academic disciplines. The total acceleration in the six years has resulted in the completion at the end of the 11th grade of all material normally covered in secondary school

and a good deal more. Thus the 12th grade material is what is normally considered to be college level . . .

ENGLISH: . . . students cover more ground more intensively than unselected divisions . . . At grade 12 the program resembles the usual freshman college course . . . Major emphasis is upon frequent writing of themes . . .

LANGUAGES: . . . a modern language or Latin is started in grade 7 and continued for six years. A second language may be selected later from among French, Italian, Spanish, German, and Russian . . .

MATHEMATICS: The normal programs for grades 7 and 8 are covered in grade 7 . . .

Grade 8: Elementary algebra—modernized course

Grade 9: Intermediate algebra—modernized course

Grade 10: SMSG geometry

Grade 11: Topics as needed in solid geometry, analytical trigonometry, study of functions, permutations, combinations, probability, theory of equations, limits, analytical geometry—line, conic sections, locus.

Grade 12: Analytical geometry and calculus

SCIENCE:

Grades 7 and 8: Material usually covered in grade 9 general science and part of high school physics.

Grade 9: Biology with biochemical approach

Grade 10: Chemistry with chemical-bond approach

Grade 11: Modern physics

Grade 12: First semester, biochemistry at the cellular level; second semester, advanced physics

SOCIAL STUDIES: No change in the usual sequence of offerings, but at each level independent research is stressed. All topics are covered in far greater depth than usual.

It is significant to note that in the six years in which this program has been offered (by outstanding teachers) discipline problems among these students have been practically nonexistent. This has been due partially to the fine teaching, but undoubtedly the quality of the program has contributed to an appreciable extent. The program carries great prestige among students and the participants take immense pride in being part of it.

With rapid learners good teaching and good guidance normally guarantee good discipline. Well planned, intelligently executed lessons, with plenty of meat in the content, a pleasant but firm manner in guiding the class, and a reasonable judgment will prevent most of the usual classroom problems. The remaining difficulties can be handled administratively. The teacher may be dismayed by all of these recommendations for working with special types of students. His attitude may be "How can I do all this?" He should bear in mind that any analysis of what is done in teaching *any* group can look formidable when put into print. Effective teaching is one of man's highest achievements, not simply an easy way to make a living!

7

Managing Large Groups

The lunchroom was crowded. Three hundred adolescents were finishing the eager business of eating and preparing for a few minutes of social release before returning to the classrooms. With varying degrees of success, some of the tables were being cleared of debris. A group of older boys was walking away from one table still covered with mealtime remnants. Mr. Smith stopped them and ordered them back. Something about his tone and manner stirred resentment in the group. Slowly they returned and went through the motions of obedience. A good deal of the mess remained as they started toward the trash cans. The teacher angrily grabbed the last of them by an arm.

"You!" he shouted. "Pick up every scrap on that table."

"It isn't mine," was the indignant reply.

This fairly normal reaction only served to add fuel to the already healthy fire.

"Get going before I clean the table with you for a rag!" the teacher retorted.

The students in the vicinity stopped talking and began to close in. They had been a crowd but now they were becoming a mob. The teacher had provided a cause to unite them. The two performers in the tense little drama faced each other, fully aware of the audience around them, and each bristled with righteous indignation.

Fortunately for both, the principal happened to enter the cafeteria at that moment. Sensing the situation immediately, he moved quickly in.

"Oh, Mr. Smith," he called loudly (and pretending not to be aware of what was going on), "there's a long-distance call for you in the office. I'll relieve you while you answer it."

Reluctantly Mr. Smith left. The principal smiled blandly at the students and glanced at the tables.

"Let's clean up for the next group," he said. "You wouldn't want to eat at these tables, would you?"

Then he began to pick up some of the papers and to chat with the students nearest to him about the forthcoming ball game. The spell was broken, the mob became a crowd again, and the bell rang for the end of the lunch period just as the tables had been cleared. Later in the day a conference followed between principal and teacher to review the circumstances and to point out how the situation might have been avoided. This particular large group problem happened in the cafeteria. It might have happened anywhere. When large groups of student gather under informal conditions and are not held together as a common class or a common club, techniques for maintaining good order differ somewhat from those employed in the classroom.

Incidents like this are *caused.* Sometimes the causes are as simple as they were in the sample above. Sometimes they are complicated and obscure. Something turns a collection of individuals into an ugly, purposeful mob. That something can and must be controlled by school authorities.

The principal in the illustration acted quickly and intuitively, drawing on his experience and training. Let us review very briefly what he actually did.

1. He shifted the attention of the group quickly away from the cause.
2. He aroused the basic decency of the individuals with a short, familiar appeal to fair play and good manners.
3. He restored a friendly atmosphere.

That was all that was necessary in this case because the provocation was petty and unnecessary. When incidents have deeper emotional ties they are not as easy to control.

Adolescents grouped together differ in several significant ways from groups of adults. They are far more easily excited by trivial matters and welcome any incident that provides a change from routine. Their values are different from and often at cross purposes to those of adults. They clearly live in a society which borders only slightly on the society of teachers and parents. Unless a teacher understands this, he will find it difficult to handle large groups of adolescents. Fortunately, they are more conditioned to the symbols of authority, at least while participating in a school function. It is usually possible to bring them under control by a firm display of authority and an appeal to such basic values as school spirit and fair play which they share with the larger society of adults. On the other hand, it is futile to attack their values while attempting to control an incident.

For instance, to continue our cafeteria example, adolescents may find it very amusing when a fellow student drops a tray or a bottle of milk on the cafeteria floor. They may even respond with a mass cheer. They mean no particular harm, and the one who has dropped the tray may even find gratification in the attention. A teacher on the scene, applying his own standards, will feel that this is an unnecessary display of bad manners, but he cannot change the customs of the entire group at the same time he is trying to restore order. If he shows anger and attempts to lecture the group at a time like this, he is asking for trouble. It would be far wiser to ignore the noise and to help the student who is in trouble. Everything will quickly return to normal.

Let us examine some of the more common situations involving large groups of students under the control of the school.

THE CAFETERIA

Secondary schools seem to have more minor disciplinary problems in connection with the cafeteria than any other place where large groups are brought together. Mealtime is certainly not the time for oppressive supervision or a Gestapo atmosphere. Students are entitled to eat their lunches in a pleasant, relaxed atmosphere and to sit with their friends for a few minutes of social conversation. On the other hand, adolescents are quite careless about picking up their after-lunch debris so some supervision is essential. If possible, when the weather permits, it is most desirable to permit them to go outdoors for a few minutes after eating. A pleasant lunch period can increase the effectiveness of classes for the rest of the day.

At the beginning of the school year, the principal should set the tone for the entire process by discussing the problems of his particular cafeteria with the teachers who have been assigned to supervise. New teachers should be carefully instructed in all the ground rules and in the methods of supervision. "He who governs least governs best" is certainly sound advice in this phase of teaching work.

Some educators believe that cafeteria supervision should not be a normal part of any teacher's duties. They feel that this is more or less a police function and is not a fitting task for a professional teacher. Others feel that it is part of the educative process and that teachers are far more capable of indoctrinating students to respect the rights of others than any non-professionals who may be hired for the purpose. In most schools this is an academic question since only teachers or student monitors are available for the task. Some schools rely partially on student supervisors, selecting students who are respected by their peers. Frequently a student service organization such as a varsity club or a football club undertakes to help the school in this way. No student should, however, be asked to report a fellow student for minor infractions of rules. This violates a fundamental taboo of adolescent society and places the student monitor in a very difficult position.

At least one responsible adult should be in charge at all times. This usually is a teacher. If a serious accident were to occur in a student-supervised cafeteria, it is doubtful whether a court would find this reasonable supervision. A lawsuit would more likely result in a finding of negligence on the part of the school. This must be borne in mind by the principal who is ultimately responsible for the safety and well-being of students in his school.

Many problems in school cafeterias can be prevented by an efficient organization of services. Students who carry lunches should be able to buy milk without going through the hot lunch lines. Trash cans should be conveniently located and should be emptied frequently to avoid overflow. Students should be able to return their trays and dishes without waiting in long lines. The temptation is great to abandon dishes when faced with the prospect of a long wait to return them.

The lunch schedule itself can make the difference between a good lunch program and perpetual misery. Secondary schools cannot ordinarily afford the old-fashioned luxury of closing down all operations for an hour to permit everyone to go home for lunch. Even the uncrowded school must feed its students in shifts. Cafeterias are expensive to build and must be planned for more uses than that of providing a place for the entire school to eat at one time. The average school cannot seat half its population in the cafeteria at one time. This means three or more lunch periods are often required in order to accommodate everyone comfortably.

The time required to move a group of students from their classrooms to the cafeteria or back will vary from school to school, but each trip will require a minimum of two to three minutes in all but the smallest schools. The lunch period itself will require a minimum of twenty minutes, not counting travel time. Thus a three-shift lunch process will consume at the very least a sixty-eight minute period with one-third of the school splitting a class in the middle for lunch. Most schools are reluctant to move from two to three shifts for this reason. The inconvenience of the split period offsets the convenience of an uncrowded cafeteria. Eventually, however, the combination of a short lunch period and a crowded cafeteria, forces the school to make the move.

Once a school is forced into a three-shift lunch, it should investigate the advantages of multiple stage scheduling or, as it is sometimes called, free-flow scheduling. Under this system, the school is moved in and out of the cafeteria in many stages. The first group arrives, filling a portion of the cafeteria. Then the second group arrives, after the first group has settled down to eat. Similarly, a third group arrives. By now the first group has nearly finished its lunch period, the second one is halfway through its meal, and the third one is just starting. As the first one leaves by one door, a fourth group is coming in another door, and so it goes throughout the entire period with three or four groups in the cafeteria at all times, but in different stages of eating. This eliminates the need for long lines and expedites every process up to the return of trays and dishes. It also prevents the problem of an entire cafeteria filled with students with nothing to do for several minutes.

Activities requiring preparation before and clean-up after class such as physical education, art, home economics, industrial arts, and laboratories, can be scheduled first or last to avoid the splitting of these periods. It is true that some classes may convene for a few minutes, adjourn for lunch, and then reconvene for a longer period. Once students and teachers become accustomed to this it creates no particular hardship. Any given class consists of several phases and this type of lunch schedule merely calls for a little organization.

The free-flow system is particularly popular in large schools or in medium sized schools with limited cafeteria facilities. It actually appears to be more complicated than it is and from a disciplinary point of view it prevents potentially troublesome situations such as crowding, long lines, and formation of large groups with nothing to do.

It can easily be argued that twenty minutes is too short a lunch period, but bear in mind that we picture a *minimum* period of twenty minutes, not counting travel, and assuming the presence of no long lines for obtaining food or for disposing of trays and refuse. It would, of course, be very desirable to offer a longer period, perhaps with a brief session of informal dancing in the gym after lunch, but this is only an idle dream in the typical secondary school today. Adjustments can usually be made for students who eat very slowly or for other unusual conditions. Most adolescents arrive in the cafeteria with healthy appetites and proceed to eat in a very businesslike manner. Discipline problems occur after eating, if at all.

ATHLETIC EVENTS

Most junior high schools today prefer intramural athletics to interscholastic competition, but the latter plays an important part in the life of the average high school.

In spite of the increased emphasis on individual carry-over sports such as tennis, swimming, and golf, in which the student can participate throughout most of his life, football, basketball, and baseball continue to draw crowds of spectators in the average American high school. In general this is a wholesome situation and can have a positive influence on school discipline since school spirit and good morale among students are essential to good discipline. Furthermore, there are basic values taught by the effective coach in team play which are not present in individual sports.

The coach, as a matter of fact, emerges as a very important figure in the disciplinary picture, not merely in the control of the game itself, but as a strong influence throughout the school. He serves as an example for his athletes and, in the adolescent society, the athletes are examples for the entire school. This strategic position of the coach should not be ignored by administrators. In the game situation he is also a key figure but there he can only be responsible for the players on the field and on the bench. While it is true that their attitudes will serve as an example for the spectators, additional supervision must also be provided. Since many spectators at schoolboy games do not attend the school, the principal must take the same reasonable precautions necessary at any large public gathering. Police officers should be on duty in sufficient numbers and in strategic locations. Local experience will determine the details. Coaches should have an adequate number of assistants to handle the numerous details involved in a game. The principal or his delegated representative should be on hand in case an emergency decision must be made. Some states require a representative of the principals' association responsible for athletics to be present. A physician should be on hand or readily accessible, depending on the sport.

Unpleasant incidents at athletic contests are frequently the result of poor officiating or dereliction of duty by officials who are usually supplied by the principals' association. These officials should be carefully and fairly rated by coaches. The principal or the athletic director should check on this, since many coaches have a tendency to overrate officials when their team wins. Although the school cannot usually control the assignments, it can often refuse to accept poor ones. Due to training requirements of new officials, weak or inexperienced men must occasionally be tolerated in unimportant games, but a weak official should not be accepted for a game in which the rivalry is keen.

Spectator indoctrination. The principal must assume the ultimate responsibility for spectator training, although every teacher can share in this work. Every opportunity should be seized for this important program. Posters and mottos can be used most effectively and assembly programs should occasionally feature this type of indoctrination. Our emphasis here is not to be misconstrued as a plea to cut into the main business of education with spectator training or the raising of morale, but we do feel that the process of teaching can be best accomplished in a wholesome atmosphere where school spirit and morale are high and discipline is sound.

A college hockey coach, who is also a high school principal, recently confided to one of the authors that, in his long experience, he had never seen such poor sportsmanship displayed by college spectators toward visiting hockey teams as in one contest where he was forced to threaten to take his team off the ice unless the local authorities controlled the spectators, *who were all students of a very famous and highly selective college!* As a matter of fact, his entire schedule was being played in very well known eastern liberal arts colleges, nonsectarian and sectarian.

It would be tempting for the harassed secondary school educator to blame the colleges, and perhaps with some justification. It is clear, however, that these young men could not have learned very much about sportsmanship in high school. This type of behavior does not develop over night.

One specific way in which students can be indoctrinated in good sportsmanship is through teaching them the rules of the various sports and the finer points of play. There is really no need to do this in time that should be devoted to physics or mathematics. Occasionally, a gym class or an assembly might be devoted to an understanding and appreciation of the sport in season. A coach and some of the players might run through a few plays, perhaps in slow motion, to illustrate the techniques involved. Voluntary after-school sessions could provide the time for this enrichment. Even an athletic contest can be a dull affair to a spectator who has a limited knowledge of the rules of the game, and in today's world youngsters with mediocre athletic talent are simply not given the opportunities to play, as they used to be, in the vacant lots. Vacant lots have largely disappeared, especially in suburbia. Thus many of them come to high school with a very limited knowledge of the major sports.

Much of the booing and other forms of protest at games result from ignorance of penalty rules rather than from criticism of officials' judgments. It is possible to eliminate most booing by indoctrination but it is easier to prevent it by enlightenment.

SOCIAL EVENTS

The same basic rules which apply above also apply for all social events in the school. Students are taught about good manners and they are properly supervised to see that no slips are made. Although a school cannot control the behavior of students before and after social affairs, it can enforce reasonable rules for the parties themselves.

Dances are particularly important, and the first consideration should be for the general tone of the entire affair. The atmosphere should be pleasant but excessive informality should be discouraged. Major dances can provide the opportunity for students to learn about social customs such as reception lines. The music should be in good taste and students should be required to dress appropriately. There is no reason for school dances to cater to the lowest level of adolescent tastes.

Here are a few suggestions for regulations which many schools have found to be very practical in conducting major dances. In order to be effective, however, these rules must be fully publicized in advance of each dance and strictly enforced:

1. Each student is responsible for the conduct of his or her guest from outside the school and for the guest's advance knowledge of the rules.
2. No student or guest will be admitted later than a half-hour after the starting time of the dance, nor will he be allowed to leave earlier than the official closing time.
3. No student or guest may leave the dance on any errand and return. In case of illness or emergency, exceptions can be made and parents will be notified immediately by telephone if possible.

Here would usually follow the local regulations on dress and other matters. Chaperones should be fully aware of all these rules and should have specific instructions in regard to their duties.

Other social events which involve large groups should also be carefully supervised. The supervision need not be heavy handed or oppressive, but it must be firm. Adolescents in informal situations can exercise a good deal of self supervision but the school cannot abandon its legal responsibility. There are always a few individuals who are immature or maladjusted and will go to great lengths to be the center of attention. These attention seekers can usually be handled by diverting their energies into responsibilities connected with running the affair. The best way to deal with a comedian is to let him display his talents officially. When he has run out of material, put him to work on something else.

SCHOOL BUSES

With the increase of consolidation of secondary school districts has come a tremendous increase in school bus transportation. The buses are also being used more frequently for educational trips and athletic contests; as a result, the average student spends a good deal of time daily in waiting for or riding on them. The only adult supervision usually provided is the driver. His responsibility for safe transportation is tremendous and he usually has all he can do to attend to his driving without being concerned with problems of discipline. A bus driver does not have the training of a teacher and should not be expected to supervise his passengers in transit.

It is to be expected that a school bus will reflect released tensions after several hours of school. On the other hand, students must be taught to behave courteously and sensibly on buses. The driver is only human and cannot help but be distracted by shouting and confusion. He should be instructed to stop the bus immediately if the general behavior of his passengers becomes bad and not to continue until he gets complete cooperation. In the cases of individuals who are boisterous, he should take their passes and turn them in to the administration with a complete report of the incident. The student should then appear with his parents for a clarification of the incident and a warning that future misbehavior will result in a loss of riding privileges.

Many states do not require the provision of free bus transportation for high school students. If this is the case, and transportation is still provided, it should be regarded as very much of a privilege. In any event, misbehavior on a bus in transit should be regarded as a serious matter since it may endanger the lives of all the passengers as well as the driver. A harassed and confused bus driver cannot operate efficiently.

It is generally considered good practice to handle bus discipline at the education department rather than at the school level. This results in greater consistency and efficiency. By the time youngsters have reached grade seven, all but the maladjusted have been thoroughly trained in school bus behavior. If they have had no previous experience the school should take the time to explain the rules and the reasons for them. The safety record of American school buses is a good one, but even one accident is one too many.

ASSEMBLIES

An assembly program can be the cohesive force that unites a school and, particularly in schools fortunate enough to be able to seat the entire student body at one time, it has a great potential for raising morale and school spirit. An assembly is, in a sense, the principal's classroom where he can teach a great many things if he has the special skills required for communication with large groups of youngsters.

The assembly program can also be a potential volcano ready to erupt with mass displays of bad manners, boredom, and ill concealed restlessness. This is not always a sign of a poorly run school, but it is nearly always a sign of poor planning, at least for the program that caused the eruption. Here are a few suggestions for preventing discipline trouble in school assemblies:

1. Try to seat students by homerooms or by classes and ask their teachers to sit with them. Do not permit students to seek out their friends in getting seated, for this can be as troublesome in the auditorium as it is in the classroom. Teachers should not ordinarily stand watching the students during the program, for this creates a poor atmosphere and makes a bad impression on visitors. A competent teacher can spot a potential heckler from a considerable distance, even while seated.
2. Set the tone of the assembly by a brief opening exercise,

preferably of a patriotic and religious nature. A flag salute or the singing of a patriotic song, or both, is very satisfactory, followed by a moment of silent prayer or a recitation of the Lord's Prayer where local usage permits.

3. Plan the programs carefully with student participation and faculty supervision. Programs which merely entertain should be forbidden. Adolescents are easily bored, but they should be taught to be bored politely. Sugar-coated assembly programs are no more justifiable than sugar-coated classes. On the other hand, there is no point in seeking out dullness of material or delivery merely to teach polite boredom.

Student performers should not be permitted to appear merely because they wish to have a showcase for their alleged talents. They should measure up to a reasonable standard of quality. Let the untalented singers perform at home for their appreciative parents, but make a real effort to seek out genuine student talent. Adolescents take pride in the accomplishments of their fellow students as singers, dancers, instrumentalists, actors, or speakers.

Guest speakers and even paid performers should also be carefully selected. Not many adults have the knack of speaking to students, and some who have the gift have very little to say. Remember that a poor speaker appearing for a worthy cause can do more harm than good for that cause.

4. Publicize the varied accomplishments of students by suitable public recognition. Letter awards to athletes are very appropriate providing they are not all crowded into one lengthy assembly at the end of the year. Try to close each sport season with a brief awards assembly. In this way the recognition of each athlete is not overshadowed by the length of the program and the number of awards.

We should also remember that there are many other areas of accomplishment besides athletics. Even the large school can find time for a public recognition of major scholarship winners and other academic achievements. There is no shortage of prizes and some discrimination should be exercised in their selection. Essay contests, for example, have become so numerous that the National Association of Secondary School Principals has been obliged to screen them. If the average high school were to sponsor every essay contest urged on them, students would be writing essays from September to June! This is not to say that the volunteer who wins a major essay contest should not receive public recognition. Students like to feel they are part of a going concern and they know that their school's reputation is made in many varied fields of endeavor.

5. Assemblies can be closed effectively with a brief ceremony dedicated to pride in the school. Many schools have developed a school creed which is recited in unison by students in assemblies. Almost every school has a song which can be a very fitting closing for an assembly.

Assemblies, social events, athletic contests, and lunch periods —any event which brings large numbers of students together, reflects the general spirit and morale of the school. Poor morale leads to poor behavior, but even students in excellent schools with the very highest morale must be supervised with intelligence, foresight, and understanding. The larger share of this responsibility rests with the principal, but every teacher and every employee of the school must contribute to the team effort.

8

Attendance Problems

It is appealing to contemplate the school of tomorrow in which personnel, program, and plant will be combined to create a meaningful, well-rounded experience for every child, and in which there will be no need for an attendance officer. Strong motivation from within will eliminate attendance and tardiness problems along with all other concerns with discipline. In the meantime, the teacher and the administrator must work in the school of today in which truancy, class cutting and tardiness are annoying and very real portions of the disciplinary picture.

REASONS FOR ADMINISTRATIVE CONCERN

Truancy, or hooky, is part of American folklore. From *Tom Sawyer* to modern comic strips, mature Americans have chuckled over the ingenious efforts of healthy American boys to reject the tortures of the classroom in favor of the pastoral delights of the old swimming hole. When we free our minds of the mist of nostalgia, however, we face a day in which torture has disappeared from the classroom and concrete has surrounded the filtered waters of the average swimming hole. Frequently the swimming hole is housed in the school itself, complete with coaches, locker rooms, and showers. But truancy, alas, is still with us.

The basic problem is simple. You cannot help a child who is absent from school. Attendance must be a serious concern of the school administration for at least three important reasons:

1. Academic difficulties. A student who manages to obtain passing grades in spite of frequent absences is a barometer indicating a storm warning. Something is wrong! Either the teachers are spending too much time in repetition like the radio soap operas of yesterday which were paced to be followed by sporadic listening, or the sometimes student is taking a course far below his ability level.

Most students experience academic trouble in direct proportion to the number of their absences. The school may have an excellent make-up system with all teachers available for help after school, but the most effective way to avoid this type of trouble is to crack down on unnecessary absence and tardiness. No school wants a student to attend when he is ill. He could endanger his own health as well as the health of others. On the other hand, secondary school students should be taught that their school work is their primary job and that it has priority over dental appointments which can be made after school, shopping trips, helping mother prepare for her bridge luncheon, and the countless other frivolous reasons which keep students out of school from time to time—often with the full approval of their parents.

The final decision on the merits of an excuse for absence must be the school's. Unless the parents provide suitable alternatives (suitable not merely to the parents, but to the authorities) such as approved tutoring or private schooling, the compulsory attendance laws require them to send their children to school whenever it is in session and not at their convenience. This means that barring mental or physical illness, unusual hardships such as unreasonable or dangerous travel where no free transportation is provided, or other genuine emergencies, they must see to it that their children attend school every day and on time. In cases of differences of opinion as to any of these factors, the burden of proof is on the parents and the final judgment rests with the court. Since state laws vary in detail, the school administration is expected to have a thorough understanding of the attendance laws of his state as well as local ordinances and policies.

Many schools have found it useful to publicize these laws through the usual channels from time to time, along with the regular requests for cooperation in the matter of attendance. Care should be taken, however, to avoid the impression that broadside threats are being made.

2. **Truancy as a symptom.** Frequent truancy is often a sympton of maladjustment. Court records all over the country show a high correlation between delinquency and truancy. This implies that although the school must deal directly with truancy as a breach of discipline, it should also look to the home and, perhaps, to some other agency for assistance in severe cases. The single incident can be dealt with by routine punishment, but frequent truancy should call for a parent conference. First, however, the absences should be checked to see if a pattern exists. It may be that the student is simply avoiding some class such as physical education. Perhaps he cannot face the prospect of being ridiculed in the shower room because of a physical abnormality. Occasionally an investigation will quickly reveal the cause of the problem and make possible relatively simple remedial action.

If the truancy persists, and all efforts fail to stop it in the case of a student under sixteen, the school may have to turn to the Juvenile Court for assistance. Truancy, in itself, is sufficient cause for court referral and often the court has resources to correct the situation which are unavailable to the school.

3. **Employers and attendance records.** Administrators know that almost all large-scale employers are very much inter-

ested in the school attendance records of job candidates. To them poor school attendance is predictive of poor job attendance, and is also a symptom of unreliability in general. Even if poor health is the reason, they are not interested in the youngster, for a sickly employee can be very expensive today due to the prevalence of liberal sick leave policies in business and industry.

It is not enough that administrators and teachers are aware of all this. The students must also know, and simply telling them is not enough. It is far more effective to post on the bulletin board the actual forms used by employers, with a red circle pencilled around the attendance line. This concentration on attendance is usually more important with girls, and companies which employ large numbers of girls and women frequently want to know the exact numbers of tardinesses, absences, and dismissals. Telephone company and insurance company forms make excellent propaganda devices for this purpose.

THE ADMINISTRATIVE APPROACH

The principal and his staff should devote a portion of their daily time to a continuous effort to improve attendance. Attacks should be made on all fronts and the pressure should be constant. Some schools have found that a concentrated drive following a period of routine efforts brings amazing results. The obvious conclusion must be that the drive should be sustained.

We have pointed out that a propaganda campaign can be helpful in improving attendance. If no time is available for the preparation of posters and displays, ready-made posters can be purchased at a reasonable price. Outside speakers, especially personnel executives, can also help the cause, especially if they are brought in to speak to smaller groups so that the stage can be set for discussion and questioning. Attendance records should, of course, only represent a portion of such a discussion, but they should not be neglected.

Dealing with parents. The key figures in the campaign for better attendance are parents. Without their cooperation, the school cannot hope for success. Most parents want good attendance records for their children and many of them are eager to cooperate, but there are some who do not care and a few who actually conspire with their children to remain out of school for trivial reasons. Almost any attendance officer has had the experience of a mother's lying to him about her child's absence even to the point of saying that he is in the home ill when, in truth, she has no idea of his whereabouts. This is a sad situation and the only way to deal with it is to lay the cards on the table. Threats of court action sometimes get results. If not, the school should refer the parents for legal action, since they are breaking the law.

Courts are usually inclined to side with the schools in matters of attendance and are not disposed to release parents from their obligations because of legal technicalities. The most common penalty is a fine and often repeated offenses will result in the child being taken from the custody of the parents and assigned to a state school. Courts have even upheld the rights of school systems to require physical examinations, inoculations, and similar public health precautions, individual religious views to the contrary notwithstanding. Compulsory flag salutes which conflict with religious beliefs have not been upheld, however. Thus, a pupil who is excluded for failure to salute the flag for religious reasons may not be referred for court action due to failure to attend school.

Care should be taken not to lose the cooperation of parents in general by needlessly antagonizing them. When they are contacted on a question of attendance or tardiness, they should be given the impression that this is a routine procedure which is initiated solely in the best interests of the student. If a parent becomes angry because he feels that his judgment is being questioned, it should be remembered that this is a normal reaction for some people. He will usually respond favorably to courteous treatment.

The importance of accurate records. When a home is called by telephone or directly by an attendance officer and a later check reveals that the student was erroneously reported absent by a teacher or clerk, a great deal of harm has been done. The story will be repeated by the parents to their circle of friends, causing considerable loss of face for the school. Conversely, when a truant is marked present by error, a red herring has been dragged across the trail. School attendance records have the status of official documents and should be maintained with the greatest care. They may even determine the outcome of legal actions. Carelessness should not be tolerated by the administration, and when it is found that a teacher is habitually remiss in this phase of his work, the principal should try to emphasize the importance of improvement.

Clerks are usually more accurate than teachers in maintaining routine records since they are not distracted by the many and varied professional duties of teachers. Many schools, particularly larger ones, have found it expedient to have the official registers maintained by a clerk. If this is the case, the clerk should be trained to look for patterns in absences and tardiness and to call them to the attention of the appropriate disciplinary officer. Such a clerk quickly learns the names of students who must be watched, and may even be assigned to make the routine telephone checks when disciplinary officers are absent.

Special cases. Many special circumstances lead to absence and tardiness and may call for special handling by the school. The openings of hunting or fishing seasons often result in a long absentee list. Most schools accept this philosophically if only one day is involved, but a student who is in severe academic trouble can ill afford the luxury of time off for fly casting. He should be taught that the leisure activities of life are earned by honest work on his main job—in this case going to school.

The family trip to a palm-shaded beach can be a real headache in northern schools since it often involves a number of days or even weeks. It would be unfair to issue *carte blanche* exemption for students who are fortunate enough to have parents who can afford such a trip. On the other hand, it would be equally unfair to penalize these students arbitrarily, since they usually have no control over the situation. A compromise can often be effected in which the burden of make-up is on the student and no teacher is required to provide free tutoring for these people. The parents should also be told that very probably the student's grades will suffer as a result of the absence.

Occasionally older boys request time off for military reserve training duty, usually of two weeks duration. The principal should know that all reserve units try to schedule their training periods to coincide with school vacations. Any training period during the school year is optional and voluntary and may be vetoed by the principal. A telephone call or a letter to the student's commanding officer will verify this. A judgment should, of course, be based on the school record of the student and on the nature of the training. In some cases, the latter may be more valuable than equivalent time spent in school. In any case, the principal should bear in mind that no military reserve organization wants to interfere with the school work of one of its members. A high school graduate is far more valuable to them than a drop-out.

Sometimes unusual family circumstances require a student to be absent or tardy frequently. An invalid mother, a marginal family farm, or the necessity for a student to contribute to the actual support of his family would be examples of this sort.

The school should make an effort to determine the true facts of the case and, in worthy situations, temper justice with mercy. An appropriate entry can also be made in the student's permanent record card so that a future employer would not be misled by his attendance record.

Inclement weather. Bad weather, particularly in northern states, can have a disastrous effect on attendance. Secondary school students, and particularly high school students, should be hardier than their younger brothers and sisters. Inclement weather should keep them home only when road conditions are hazardous. By and large, the weather conditions which keep them from school should be bad enough to keep their fathers home from the plant or the office. Judgment should be exercised. The frequently absent student who stays home because of a rainstorm should not be excused. When the weather is bad, the principal can usually predict the names of the students who will appear and those who will fail to make it.

The school should have some facilities for drying wet clothing, even if it is merely a space next to the boilers. It would not be unreasonable to have a dryer in the home economics suite for students with soaked clothing, especially those who live a long way from the school.

Illness. One of the important reasons for telephone checks on absentees would be to offer assistance, particularly in the case of lengthy illness. It is, therefore, a good idea to check all the absentees from time to time and not merely the ones with poor attendance records. If the student is well enough to do some schoolwork, books and assignments can be sent home by neighboring students. Some schools even have provisions for home teachers to provide tutoring.

Make-up policies. When a student is truant or is tardy without a good reason, he should not have the privilege of making up any work he may have missed. Some schools carry this further and recommend that teachers assign a zero for the classes missed even though no grades were given for that day. All of this may seem excessive to some as well as contradictory to the policy of not levying academic penalties as punishment. The particular offense is unique, however, and must be dealt with realistically. The academic penalty, if coupled with a sensible marking procedure which does not attempt to measure a student's progress like a bin of wheat, can be most effective. If make-up is permitted after truancy, it will tend to minimize the seriousness of the offense, especially if other penalties are omitted in favor of a parent conference. Truancy must be viewed as a matter of grave concern.

A student who is habitually truant is probably failing or close to failure in most of his subjects. While it is true that he must suffer the just consequences of his actions, one must not shut off hope of improvement until it is absolutely necessary. The motivation for improvement requires the knowledge that a changed attitude plus sustained effort for a reasonable period will result in improved grades.

All make-up policies should be elastic enough to permit the teacher to exercise judgment in individual cases, and no student should feel that in March or April he is hopelessly lost because his average is so low that he must do one-hundred percent work for the rest of the year in order to pass. A sincere willingness to learn, honest work for two or three months, and a passing grade on the final examination should tip the scale in favor of a passing grade. No human being should be deprived of hope. *A very common source of discipline trouble is the student who feels that he has reached the point of no return in a given subject.* This student must be helped with proper guidance. Once he agrees to the proposition that he must eventually pass the subject, either in summer school or regular session, he can be shown that everything he learns now will make it easier for him the next time around. It can also be pointed out to him that degrees of failure sometimes are significant to the person evaluating a record. It may be assumed by some that the student who drops to a complete failure is a quitter.

The increasing number of summer schools being operated by public school systems has opened up even further avenues of hope for floundering students. Schools with summer sessions frequently distinguish between high and low failures in assigning the number of daily hours of class. This can motivate the failing student even very late in the year to bring his average up to a point where he is eligible for a regular one hour per day course rather than a two hour double-header. Summer schools also offer hope to the students who desire to graduate with their classes. This has contributed to better morale and better discipline in the regular sessions. Where there is a possibility of success there is hope, and where there is hope there is better discipline.

Cutting classes. Secondary schools usually require attendance to be taken in every class as well as in the morning. The teacher checks the class attendance against the daily absentee list and turns in the names of students who are missing from class and not recorded as absent for the day. Carelessness in handling this detail is an invitation to cuts.

The teacher can, of course, prevent most cuts by making his classes interesting and by concentrating reasonable attention on individuals. A student who cuts a class is risking punishment in order to avoid what to him may be a greater punishment. Perhaps he has been ridiculed in front of his friends. Perhaps he feels hopelessly frustrated academically. He may merely be taking advantage of laxity in taking attendance. Students who persist in cutting classes should be treated as habitual truants, since constant cutting is a form of truancy.

Tardiness. The school should reserve the right to judge the adequacy of tardiness excuses. With some students tardiness is habitual and unless the disease can be checked before graduation, it will be a serious handicap to success in college, in the armed forces, or on the job. (For that matter, it could even cause trouble in an otherwise happy marriage!) Students who form the habit of tardiness should be counseled regularly and should have annoying penalties, such as detention, assigned. After a given number of offenses, parents should be called in for a conference.

Where bus transportation is available, the school should not accept excuses having to do with car trouble. Some students operate cars that require a daily miracle to make the trip to school without breaking down. Students' excuses are sometimes amusing. Here are three samples taken directly from the files of a suburban high school.

"I couldn't find my one sock."

"My uncle had the alarm clock down at the hen house."

(This one aroused the curiosity of the principal who discovered that the uncle had converted the hen house into a photographic dark room and used the alarm clock as a timer!)

"I thought it was Sunday because the street was so quiet."

The excuses should be recorded by the students on slips when they arrive, and these slips should be kept together so that when the time comes for a conference, they can be perused at a glance. The tardy student should, if possible, also bring with him a note from home if the reason for the tardiness is legitimate. If and when the parent is asked to come in for a conference, the authenticity of these and other documents can be verified.

The team approach. Whatever system is used to check on attendance, it should be practical and simple so that teamwork is possible. Everyone who deals with a case should have access to all pertinent data quickly, and procedures should be consistent to avoid duplication and confusion.

The first contact in all but the smallest schools is the clerk on duty in the main office. This person should see merely that the proper form is filled out and that all data goes through the proper channels without delay. The disciplinary officer (in smaller schools, the principal) checks the attendance list and judges the merits of tardiness excuses. He then accepts or rejects them, assigns detention, reprimands, or other punishment, and checks the names of absentees to be called. He or the clerk then makes the calls, and as a result a few cases may be turned over to the attendance department for house calls. If a school nurse is available, she may make the calls when claims of illness are doubted or when the school wishes to check on the progress of a student who is seriously ill. All significant data is turned over to the student's guidance counselor. If disciplinary action is advisable or if a parent conference is indicated, the counselor should be consulted. Two school officials should never work independently when they are dealing with the same problem of the same student.

In larger schools, the principal becomes involved when the case becomes very serious or when the counselor or disciplinary officer feels that he has exhausted his resources with little success. Weekly conferences can be extremely valuable in the cases of the most serious attendance problems. Everyone who has worked with these students should be present, including the homeroom teachers. Recent and complete reports on the work, the current attitude, and the conduct of the students should be available at this time. These cases are often quite complicated and many heads are better than one. In any event, the principal should consult with all members of the team before taking drastic action such as suspension or referral to the superintendent of schools.

THE ROLE OF THE TEACHER

It has not been intended to cast the teacher in the role of the minor player in our little drama. On the contrary, he is most important. In the first place, the quality of his teaching and his sensitivity to the needs and problems of the individual student have a direct bearing on attendance as well as on all other phases of discipline. Other members of the team must carry out the routine processes of investigation, counseling, and punishment, simply because the teacher does not have the time to do these things. A great many demands are made on his time and a wise administrator is aware of this. The teacher should not be asked to sit in on a lengthy conference when a written report will suffice, but he should be informed that he is welcome if he wishes to attend. We have pointed out that the primary purpose of the administrative team is to help the teacher do a better job in the classroom. When absence or tardiness becomes a problem with a student, the teacher may turn to the guidance department or to the administration for assistance. He is not helping them; they are helping him—for his is the main business of the school.

Absence and testing. One of the more annoying problems of the teacher is the student whose illness and absence frequently coincides with tests. His first duty is to call this to the attention of the administration. If truancy is not determined, he can do two things to discourage the continuance of this type of coincidence. First, set a strict limit on the period of grace in which a make-up test will be given, with the responsibility on the student to make the appointment for an after-school session. Secondly, prepare an alternative test which is perceptibly and legitimately more difficult than the original. Since only a few students are involved, the test might well be an essay type, requiring enough time to annoy the annoyer as well as to test his knowledge of the material. If these steps are followed consistently, "test illness" will be cut to a minimum.

Since it is entirely possible that the coincidence of testing and illness described above is genuine, the test given for make-up should be graded very carefully and not marked down because of the suspicious circumstances. If the evidence points to truancy, of course, no make-up test should be given. This is equally true of all academic problems based on poor attendance. Make-up privileges should be granted, denied, or modified in terms of the nature of the individual case with a heavy emphasis on the general attitude of the student. Whenever possible, academic penalties should be avoided.

All of the efforts directed at improving school attendance should be applied in the light of the knowledge that frequent tardiness, cutting classes, truancy, and poor attendance in general are symptoms rather than diseases. Carefully maintained records, thorough investigations into causes, and teamwork can make possible improvements in all but the most difficult cases. Efforts expended in this work are well worth while in terms of improved grades, better attitudes, and a more positive approach to the future by students affected.

9

Overcoming Plant Defects: Principal Devices

The principal glanced at his watch. Twelve-fifteen. The day was Friday. He looked over at his appointment pad. All clear until two-thirty. This was his day for a building inspection which ordinarily he would make after school, but with the third-floor students at lunch and no appointments on his calendar, he could get a good start now.

Notifying his secretary, he made for the stairway with note-pad and pencil. He saw as he started up the thirty-year-old stairway that four badly worn steps had not been replaced as he had requested. The stairs were steep, and he was secretly grateful for the excuse to pause long enough to catch his breath and to make the notation. At the top his eye caught the Victory Hop poster taped to the wall. The dance had been held a week before. The advisor should have reminded his committee to remove all posters. Another entry.

Selecting a master key, he opened and closed a dozen student lockers at random. Everything shipshape. Good. He walked into the boys' lavatory. No cigarette butts. No writing on the walls. Good custodian on the third floor. He opened a window.

The next room was the domain of an elderly but adequate teacher of shorthand. Everything was in good order but the temperature was unbearably high. Eighty-one degrees! To the teacher this was probably an ideal temperature. He started to make another notation but changed his mind and took a closer look at the thermometer. Then he took a penknife from his pocket and began to tinker with the instrument, finally sliding the tube down slightly so that it read ninety-two degrees. On his way back to the stairs he would close the windows and by that time the actual room temperature would be around seventy-two. The teacher would read eighty-two and everyone would be happy. No restless, uncomfortable students. No needless discipline referrals.

The next room housed another adequate teacher but one who became so engrossed in her mathematics that the world around her became slightly blurred. At that moment everything seemed a little blurred in that particular room for all the shades had been drawn against the morning sun which by now had disappeared over the roof. The ceiling lights were not turned on and unless something was done, students would be straining to read algebraic formulas on chalkboards and in textbooks for the rest of the afternoon. The principal sighed, raised the shades, turned on the lights, and opened the windows briefly for a change of air.

Desks full of trash were featured in the next room and another notation was made. So it went across the entire third floor. Shades were adjusted here and there and windows were opened. Notes were made for later polite memos to the teachers involved. The building was old and lacked many desirable features, but the principal was determined that his teachers use effectively what facilities they did have. Improvements would come eventually if he nagged persistently enough.

The principal of any school must work ceaselessly on these two plant problems: getting the most out of what he has, and obtaining needed improvements under a long-range priority program. He knows that the building and its equipment represent a very large investment for the school district and contribute in no small way to the quality of the educational program.

American business and industry know the value of environmental factors in increasing efficiency and productivity among workers. Millions of dollars have been spent on research in lighting, color schemes, and design of furniture in order to provide the best working conditions. The same psychological and physical factors apply to students who are people too and to schools which are places where work is done. Does it seem far-fetched to point to building and equipment inadequacies as possible sources of discipline trouble?

FACTORS AFFECTING PUPIL COMFORT

Let us examine briefly the environmental conditions which may contribute to pupil discomfort, restlessness and, in some cases, to overt misbehavior. Unless we are at least aware of them, nothing can be done to improve them.

Overcrowding. We have heard a great deal about the fact that most American secondary schools are overcrowded. Our entire nation is aware of it and is trying to do something about it, but between the time a community first accepts the idea that it must build a new school and the time the building is ready for occupancy, two or three years go by and with them the major portion of the high school life of many students. What can we do to prevent lowering standards during this period of transition?

Overcrowding creeps up slowly on a secondary school and manifests itself in many subtle ways besides the obvious problems of crowded corridors during passing periods, inadequate space in cafeterias, libraries, and laboratories. The typical older high school is divided like an egg crate into a number of identical rooms, usually equipped with forty to forty-five screwed-down desk-and-chair units. Obviously no secondary school could or would divide its classes into groups of forty-five. This number can hardly be justified for any type of teaching. It is too small for a large-group lecture, far too large for a successful discussion group, and at least fifteen over the number generally accepted as a maximum for a conventional class. A crowded school must seat its students somewhere, so usually it begins to place students with study periods at the rear of regular classes. There is little need to point out the disadvantages of this practice, especially in terms of control.

An overcrowded school is limited sharply by the number of recitation spaces. Any new course or activity, any plan to cut class sizes in certain subjects by providing more teachers always comes up against a stone wall—no place to put them. Guidance facilities needed to take care of the larger enrollment cannot be housed properly. Converting a classroom into cubicles and offices is unthinkable. In short, any of the efforts to maintain the quality of the educational program is checkmated by the plant. Unless drastic action is taken the whole program begins to deteriorate and with it goes good discipline.

The first administrative device usually applied to overcrowding is a shift in attendance areas or a redistribution of the grade structure to even off the student population over the entire system. Sometimes a crowded four year high school can become a three year school by retaining the ninth grade in one or more junior high schools. Shifts of this sort can be extremely unpopular with parents and should be made only as a part of a long-range plan—and then only if absolutely necessary.

A more promising idea is that of a staggered session. Under this plan a portion of the school, say the senior class, starts the day at an earlier time than usual. The rest of the school reports an hour or so later. The seniors are dismissed earlier. A typical schedule for a school which ordinarily runs from 8:30 to 2:30 but which is now forced into a staggered schedule might be:

7:15 Seniors report
9:10 Others report
1:15 Seniors leave
3:10 Others leave

Assuming a six-period day, we can visualize two beautifully uncrowded periods from 7:15 to 9:10, crowded conditions until 1:15, and two more uncrowded periods from 1:15 to 3:10. During the crowded portion of the day the school would plan to fill every space to capacity. At other times it would enjoy the luxury of space to spare. Seniors would also have the advantage of early dismissal for part-time work.

There are disadvantages, of course. Seniors who wish to participate in athletics, dramatics, or other after-school activities would face nearly two hours of waiting after dismissal. It would be naive to assume that they would go home for two hours of study and then return to school. If they were to remain at school, they would defeat the purpose of the staggered session. Then there are the families with two or more children in different grades. One can visualize family problems.

An even less desirable solution is the double session with the entire school divided into two shifts. This is normally done by starting one group quite early in the day and finishing the other group very late in the day. It almost always involves shortening the day for each session, cutting the exposure of each student to the educative process. Other variations on the multiple session theme have been proposed, usually by theorists: splitting the week into Group A on Mondays, Tuesdays, and Wednesdays, and Group B on Thursdays through Saturdays, with each group attending for a longer day; splitting the year into four three-month vacation periods so that at any given time a quarter of the school is out on vacation. Each of these involves a radical change in the work and vacation habits of the American people. Perhaps the high cost of school buildings may force us into some such solution, but widespread acceptance of these plans is hardly imminent.

More promising ideas include the extension of work-experience programs so that industry and business may become partners in the educative process and more flexible scheduling within the framework of a longer school day with students in the building only when they are actually using school facilities. Either way, the entire community becomes a part of the school campus with students spending portions of their school day in offices, shops, museums, libraries, and other places where learning takes place. This is, of course, a tremendous undertaking to plan and administer but many schools have made interesting starts in this direction.

Heat. In addition to the discomfort of a crowded school, there are several other factors which can combine to make school a nearly intolerable experience. One of these is too much or too little heat. Many of our older schools are poorly heated and uninsulated. In warmer climates, hot weather can be a real headache. Most business offices have accepted air conditioning as a necessity for efficient productivity, but it is still considered very much of a luxury in our schools.

More efficient heating systems and better insulation can often be sold to reluctant school boards by pointing out that they will pay for themselves over a period of time. The building principal should acquaint himself with the facts of the case for his school. It does not pay to assume that someone else is thinking about this. Often surprising things can be accomplished with facts and figures.

Teachers must take the responsibility of seeing that their rooms are comfortable. Univents, radiators, and thermostats are not nearly as difficult to deal with as the pot-bellied stoves of the earlier schoolhouses. The goal should be a uniform temperature of around 72 degrees. Bear in mind that one student gives off as much heat as about a square foot of radiation, so it makes sense to start the morning and afternoon sessions with a rapid change of air via open windows and a room temperature a couple of degrees below the ideal seventy-two.

Light. Something in our environment causes about half of us to reach voting age needing glasses. Since so many of us are exposed to schools for so many years, it is reasonable to suspect that the visual environment of classrooms may have something to do with this abnormality. Even if future research reveals that the schools are innocent of this charge, we do know that insufficient light and poor quality of light (sharp contrasts of brightness, harsh lighting, etc.) contribute perceptibly to discomfort. Engineers differ on their recommendations for ideal lighting conditions just as pediatricians differ in their recommendations for burping babies, but two conditions are all too common in most of our schools: (1) not enough artificial light is available for reading or other fine work on dark days, and (2) sharp contrasts exist between the few large lights usually in use and the darker surroundings of the classrooms.

Conditions are usually better in new schools and in older schools which have been renovated since we became aware of minimum standards for quality and quantity of lighting, but many old school buildings are still unimproved in this respect. Since 1948 most new school furniture has been finished in lighter colors, and in recent years classrooms have been painted in lighter shades rather than in the dreary hues of yesteryear. One might suspect that the paintwork of old was mixed to imitate the color of grime. Improvements in lighting are another matter, however, since most old buildings are inadequately wired. Better lighting ordinarily means complete rewiring, but the expense is well worth consideration not only in terms of the eyesight saved but also in the program improvements made possible by more power and outlets for audio-visual aids, office machines, and better cleaning equipment for custodians.

The teacher must learn to make the most of what he has available. Movable furniture can be arranged to take advantage of the existing natural and artificial light rather than to conform to arbitrary, geometric patterns of neatness. Shades, drapes, and blinds can be controlled rather than ignored. Requests can be submitted to the administration to have dirty windows washed when they become dirty rather than once a year at the convenience of the custodial staff. In short, poor lighting conditions should not be suffered in silence or ignored stoically. Too much is at stake.

Ventilation. A stuffy classroom can stifle the finest teaching. A good lesson requires oxygen for survival. Over a century ago when we were turning to Germany for leadership in pedagogy, a German expert recommended a minimum turnover of air per pupil in terms of so many cubic feet per minute. Well intentioned legislatures in some of our states wrote this into building codes for schools. Ignoring the fact that all existing building materials constantly leak air and that the large windows popular in schools are equivalent to good-sized holes in the wall, these laws led to requirements for cumbersome artificial ventilation systems. Most older schools have these systems but very few of them are in use. They are usually too noisy and too dusty. Many of them have been unused since their installation. The teacher still has one obvious source of fresh air—opened windows. Winter and summer, windows should be opened, at least briefly now and then for a change of air. The new teacher should develop this habit. It can prevent a good deal of restlessness among students.

Sound. A fairly recent development in school architecture is the science of acoustical engineering. When a teacher who has worked for years in high-ceilinged echo chambers with hard plaster, parallel walls is transferred to a new school finished with acoustical tile, he is astounded by the ease of communication and by his lack of fatigue at the end of a school day. His students, without realizing it, share his feeling of well-being. Another discordant note that contributes to restless irritation has been removed.

Improved acoustical conditions can be readily provided by the installation of inexpensive tile in almost any area. Sometimes slight building modifications must also be made to break up the reverberation patterns. The total program may be designed to isolate noisy activities from adjoining rooms and to provide acoustical comfort within each room. First consideration should be given to music rooms, auditoriums, and cafeterias. After this a high priority should be given to the classrooms where pupils spend so much of their time.

Often a teacher can effect improvements while he is waiting for the reconditioning program to catch up with his room. Here are a few suggestions addressed directly to the teacher:

1. Learn to pitch and modulate your voice to the actual conditions of your room with students in it. Don't use any more volume than absolutely necessary. A loud voice in a poorly built room adds to the discomfort of everyone listening.
2. Find by trial and error the best spot to speak from. It may be from a corner rather than from front center. Ask the students to help you. They are in a better position to judge than you are.
3. If your room is equipped with movable furniture, try moving it. Remember that hearing conditions *and* light should be considered. If you are separated from the next room by a temporary or movable partition, you and your neighboring colleague will probably want to operate from opposite ends of your rooms in order to provide the maximum distance between each other.

4. Sometimes street noises can be partially sealed out by elastic putty fitted around some of the window edges (not all of them or you will lose control of ventilation), inexpensive drapes, or storm windows.

Furniture. Secondary school students, even in the same grade, vary tremendously in size. The teacher may have students in a given class ranging in height from four feet to well over six feet and from sixty pounds to well over two hundred. It is not logical to expect them to sit at identical desks in identical chairs. The furniture in each room should be checked with a yardstick. If it is movable and identical, it may be possible to exchange a few units for larger and smaller sizes. The chief points to check are the heights of the seats from the floor and the heights above the seats of the lower portions of the desks. Even if the furniture is fixed to the floor, adjustments can sometimes be made. The point is that one or two seats should be available in sizes an inch smaller and larger than the others to accommodate unusually small or large students. If small-tablet arm chairs are in use, it is normal to have on hand one or two left-handed models. Small-tablet units should not be used in regular classrooms if it can be avoided, since they cause abnormal twisting of the spine if a great deal of writing is done on them.

Teachers are sometimes consulted in the selection of new furniture. Principals frequently are.

Here are some points to bear in mind from the viewpoint of comfort:

1. Each pupil's feet should rest flat on the floor, supporting a portion of his weight so that there is no pressure under his thighs. This requires differing seat heights in each room. Tables are readily available from manufacturers suggesting seat heights for various ages.

2. The seat should slope slightly to the rear to overcome the

tendency to slide forward and there should be room at the back for buttocks spill-out.

3. There should be no pressure under the knees.
4. There should be free space in back of the inside angle of the knees.
5. There should be free space between the upper thighs and the bottom of the desk.
6. The back edge of the desk should overlap the front edge of the chair.
7. The chair back should support the hollow of the back.
8. The desk top should be higher than the elbow with the arm hanging straight down.

These factors have, of course, solely to do with pupil comfort. Other factors such as weight, durability, price, etc. would be the concerns of the purchasing agent or the superintendent of schools.

Frequently we overlook the obvious. Discipline problems can sometimes be traced to something as simple as an uncomfortable, ill-fitting chair and desk.

SITE PROBLEMS

Today, an important consideration in the selection of a school site is the availability of a large tract of inexpensive land. Fortunately this policy also tends to minimize traffic hazards, noises, and the proximity of such attractive nuisances as candy stores with pin-ball machines and juke boxes, pizza parlors, and hot-dog stands. Such is not usually the case with older buildings. They were placed in a central location, usually in the downtown district and on as small a site as possible. This was fine in the days of the Model T, but it is hardly convenient in the age of the two-car garage. The opening and closing of the downtown high school is accompanied by traffic congestion and varying degrees of hazards for students and faculty in crossing nearby streets. A shortage of parking space is also common.

The school administration is responsible for reasonable precautions and safety indoctrination of students. Adolescents have a tendency to forget the safety habits they were so carefully taught in elementary school. At least one teacher should be responsible for conditions around the building before and after school, especially the loading and unloading of buses. Students who disregard safety rules should be reported and handled as disciplinary cases. There can be no compromise with traffic safety.

The temptations of a central location are many and varied. Periodic checks of the neighborhood youth oases should be made during school hours by administrators or teachers who are available for this duty. It pays to enlist the cooperation of the proprietors of these places rather than to treat them as corrupters of youth. If they refuse to admit students during school hours, the task of the school becomes much easier.

SAFETY IN THE SCHOOL

Safety and good discipline go hand in hand. A good many accidents can be traced to horseplay and boisterous behavior. Students who are unaccustomed to restraint in large groups can hardly be expected to cooperate in emergency drills or in the emergency itself. The connection is obvious. Safety is one of the important by-products of sound discipline in any school.

One person, preferably an administrator, should have the overall control of emergency drills. Fire and civil defense drills simply cannot be treated as routine nuisances. Every teacher and student should be thoroughly trained in these procedures. Drills should be held at various times and under various conditions. Obstructions should be introduced to condition students to using alternate routes in cases of emergency. The strictest rules should be rigidly enforced during all drills. No talking should be permitted during the exit portion of fire drills. Reentry may be conducted under more relaxed conditions to take advantage of the opportunity to let the students relax a bit. Drills should be timed and everyone notified of the results. Students should be impressed with the importance of remaining calm, following instructions, and moving quickly but not in frantic haste. Seconds may mean lives when the chips are down.

An occasional survey of safety hazards within a building is necessary because conditions constantly change. Worn stair treads do not improve as time goes by and often go unnoticed long after they have become dangerous. Furniture and equipment are sometimes stored in passage areas temporarily—and left there indefinitely. All of these things should be checked periodically and methodically. This leads to an obvious conclusion—one person should have the responsibility.

Just as industry has organized safety under the supervision of a safety engineer, the school can appoint a teacher as a safety director. A boys' physical education teacher is a logical candidate since he has had training in the prevention of injuries and is more likely to be safety-conscious than the academic teacher. In a very large school he should have a reasonable adjustment made in his schedule, and he should be encouraged to attend safety conferences as they become available. Some suggested responsibilities of the safety director would be:

1. To survey hazardous locations and to minimize danger with requests for appropriate paint and light.
2. To make students and faculty safety conscious in and around the building.
3. To report promptly all conditions not conducive to safety and to follow through on the correction of these conditions.

4. To check the conditions of fire extinguishers, hoses, fire escapes, and other related equipment and to instruct students and teachers in their use.

As we analyze each factor in preventing discipline trouble, the temptation is great to overstate the importance of each. They are all important, but we cannot contend that pupil comfort is as important as good teaching. We do maintain that to ignore pupil comfort is a singularly unintelligent approach to teaching. It is about as sensible as running a hundred-yard dash in overshoes. Yet so many teachers pay so little attention to heat, light, ventilation, noise control, and seating comfort in the classroom! One wonders if these people resent the housekeeping aspects of pedagogy because they feel that they somehow detract from the professional status of teaching. Nothing can lose face for a teacher faster than a roomful of squirming, unhappy adolescents, and so little time and effort are necessary to prevent physical discomfort!

10

Guidance, Discipline, and Policy Making

We have repeatedly emphasized the teamwork which is essential to the maintenance of a healthy, disciplinary climate in the secondary school. It should be pointed out that there are really two aspects to this teamwork—cooperative formulation of policy, and the cooperative efforts to carry out that policy. While it is true that in a democratic school system every teacher and administrator participates to some degree in the formulation of policy, the leadership and the initiative for carrying system-wide policy proposals to the school board and for putting into effect policies within a single school usually rests with administrators. This will be discussed below. As we consider first the work of the guidance department in school discipline, we will emphasize its responsibilities in carrying out existing policies. Then we will analyze the role of administrators in creating policy and demonstrate how discipline policies can be codified.

GUIDANCE

Those who have been closely associated with the work being carried on in secondary schools are well aware of the relationship of guidance to discipline. Through guidance, each child is assisted as far as possible toward a place in our way of life which will be commensurate with his abilities and aspirations. A successful guidance program requires that there be willing, active, and intelligent participation by all members of a school staff in such a program, and an underlying assumption is that through a thorough understanding of the individual child, a program of education can be devised to meet his particular needs and thus assist him toward becoming a good, productive citizen. All guidance has a common purpose—to assist the individual to make wise choices, adjustments, understandings, and interpretations in connection with critical situations in his life.

The most effective school guidance begins in the formative years when the child first enters school. In most school systems the responsibility rests squarely with the teacher since organized guidance services rarely go below the seventh grade. Peculiarly enough, even school systems which provide psychological testing of individuals seem to concentrate their efforts on the older students where the maladjustments are more dramatic—and usually beyond the fragmentary assistance which is available.

Although psychology and its allied sciences do not enable us to predict exactly how a child will react to every situation, it does help us to predict reasonably what his general reactions will be. In all cases of misbehavior except the most trivial we must look beneath the surface for the real motives.

When an individual is socially adjusted he is said to be normal. The normal person is, however, a fiction of convenience. Strictly speaking, no person is truly normal. Personality can be integrated but not standardized. No two people are completely alike. The myriad sources and reasons for pupil misbehavior and maladjustment make it necessary for guidance to begin with a study of the individual child.

In addition to being an individual, the child is also a social being and as such must learn to recognize that certain types of behavior are necessary in a civilized society. An aim of sound guidance is to help the child establish a balance between his rights as an individual and his duties as a member of a group. Its goal is to guide the native impulses of the child into proper channels and upon these impulses, to build the habits of a civilized life.

From these statements it can be seen that the aims of education in general are the aims of guidance. The distinction lies in the *methods* of guidance.

The role of guidance services. We have stated that guidance concerns itself with choices and adjustments. Guidance services can be easily justified in modern secondary schools by the continuing high rate of academic mortality, by the many obvious symptoms of maladjustment among students, and by the increasing complexities of almost every facet of life today. The major services offered by a sound guidance program may be listed as follows:

1. A THOROUGH STUDY OF THE INDIVIDUAL. This is the foundation of the guidance program. The school learns by testing, interviews, and teachers' appraisals as much as it can about the pupil so that it can help him to know himself and to help himself.

2. COMPETENT INDIVIDUAL AND GROUP COUNSELING. For the purpose of imparting information especially of a vocational nature, groups with similar interests can sometimes be brought together, but the most effective guidance device of all is the individual session between the student and a trained counselor. For this reason the pupil-counselor ratio in secondary schools should be 1 to 250-300 at the most. Any larger load will surely result in the neglect of many students who keep their problems to themselves.

3. INFORMATIONAL SERVICES TO STUDENTS. Students should

have ready access to recent and complete information on vocations, vocational trends, how to study, college and other post-high school educational opportunities, the armed forces, etc.

4. PLACEMENT AND FOLLOW-UP SERVICES. Placement service for full-time and part-time jobs for students deserves the efforts of a competent person who will actively seek opportunities for students or it will degenerate into a baby sitting bureau. Student volunteers can assist with clerical details.

5. INFORMATIONAL SERVICES TO FACULTY AND STAFF. A guidance department must work tirelessly for good relationships with the entire school staff. It needs a constant supply of information from teachers, and the best way to prime the pump is by providing information to teachers without waiting for formal requests.

6. RESEARCH. Although a small percentage of our larger school systems support a research office or subscribe to a cooperative research unit, the average secondary school must rely on universities and state and federal agencies for data. While this is useful in a general way, it often fails to hit the local target. Drop-out studies, follow-up studies, and various probes into the nature of the community and the student body itself can be very useful to a school. When it is possible, the guidance department should try to obtain these data for the school.

7. COORDINATION OF SCHOOL, COMMUNITY, AND HOME RESOURCES. A key word in guidance is coordination. Teamwork is as vital here as it is in the disciplinary effort—indeed it is often an integral part of discipline. Services to youth are too valuable to waste in duplication of efforts.

Records and reports. Sound discipline proceeds from a knowledge of the individual, and a knowledge of the individual requires conscientious and intelligent record keeping throughout his school career. By the time he has reached junior high school, a student's cumulative record folder should have been carefully edited to eliminate non-essential material, but should be complete in meaningful data. Opinions differ widely as to what material is significant so it would be wise to be conservative in discarding material. If, for example, a student is referred to a psychiatrist or to the juvenile court in his final years of high school, some of the early records which may have seemed extraneous to the teacher or counselor may take on a new significance. Following is a suggested outline of data to be included in a cumulative record folder, to be recorded on such forms and in such a manner as the school may find convenient. Needless to say, this material should be handled under conditions of strict security and should not be available to non-professional personnel.

The professional training of the teacher should be brought to bear on the proper interpretation of this data. Beginning teachers will want to consult with experienced counselors, however, in the application of this information to problem students in the classroom. Important clues will come to light as to *why* students behave as they do. This will help the teacher understand the reasons for misbehavior. In the matter of specific remedy, however, the teacher should work with the counselor since the latter has the time for more complete treatment. He may suggest to the teacher what he can do in response to certain behavior patterns, bearing in mind that her time is short in the classroom. At this point teamwork becomes an absolute necessity for an intelligent approach to behavior problems.

1. *Personal.* The complete name of student, date and place of birth, racial and nationality origin (this need not be controversial if it is not used in any discriminatory way. It may at some time be significant. If local law prohibits its being recorded, so be it.) Names and occupations of parents, places of birth of parents, address and telephone number of home,

marital status of parents, number and relative ages of siblings, dates of attendance at school, reason for transfer or drop-out. All of the foregoing may be essential at some time from a legal point of view since a school record of this sort is highly regarded as a legal document. The recording of pertinent personal information need not be viewed as an invasion of privacy if that information is used only for professional or legal purposes.

2. *Scholarship.* Marks in subject matter and citizenship traits, special failure reports, recorded reading and other achievement data, rank in class.

3. *Test scores and ratings.* All achievement and aptitude scores, College Entrance Examination Board scores, preferably expressed in percentiles or other understandable scales, personality ratings, interest inventories.

4. *Attendance.* Days absent, tardy, or dismissed each school year. Reasons for unusual records in this respect such as lengthy illnesses or chronic illness.

5. *Health.* In addition to the foregoing in relation to numerous absences, the following should be recorded: Childhood diseases, inoculations and vaccinations, physical disabilities and treatment history. The child's ability to see and hear should be recorded in terms understandable to a teacher rather than in medical shorthand. There should also be a clear statement as to the child's fitness for physical education and athletic competition.

6. *Anecdotal records.* Some effort should be made to develop a practical format for significant anecdotes, particularly in connection with a history of maladjustment. The anecdotal record should describe the behavior and not the impressions or opinions of the observer. An evaluative statement may follow, but should not be woven into the account itself. This type of record is much neglected and may be a very useful tool for the disciplinary officer as well as the counselor.

7. *Activities, honors, and awards.* Athletic participation, offices held, activity participation, honors awarded, are all important, particularly when the time comes to apply for admission to college.

8. *Miscellaneous.* Vocational plans, travel, employment records, etc. may also be of some value. A space should be provided for any data which may not fit into previously listed categories.

Attitudes about guidance. In the early development of formalized guidance programs, teachers generally viewed this new activity with suspicion and apprehension. This attitude has not been completely overcome. Since the success of the program rests on teamwork, every effort should be made by all who believe in this work to obtain maximum cooperation and support from the entire staff and from the community. The best way to obtain this support is through service—service to students, teachers, administrators, and the community.

The basic attitudes underlying successful guidance programs may be summarized briefly in the following statements:

1. The purposes of guidance are directly related to the purposes of the school itself.
2. Guidance is interested in the individual and his total adjustment and its object is to help the individual to know himself and to help himself.
3. School guidance services should be available to all pupils throughout their school careers.
4. Guidance is concerned with helping the teacher in the classroom and in extra-class activities by supporting her efforts to discover and to meet the needs of each student.
5. Guidance is also concerned with helping parents and the community in providing more adequate services for youth.
6. The administrator is responsible for the development and improvement of guidance services and seeks to provide ade-

quate time, materials, personnel, and in-service training to that end.

THE POLICY MAKERS

We have considered briefly the role of the guidance department as it seeks to carry out policies already in existence. A school, however, is a dynamic institution which must be prepared to change with the times and with changing conditions. Discipline, along with all other aspects of school life, is a changing phenomenon, reflecting the rapidly shifting community scene today. Policies relating to discipline often become outmoded. School regulations, like city statutes, become anachronisms with changing conditions. Thus policy evaluation and policy formulation become a continuous problem.

Who are the policy makers? A reflexive response would be "The School Board, of course." This is its legal function. A more reflective response would be slower in coming and more complex in nature. While it is perfectly true that the *power* to make policy is vested in the school board, recent history has seen changes wherein popular participation in policy formulation has broadened considerably. School boards have become sensitive to the desires of the people and have listened thoughtfully to articulate groups of citizens, to teachers, and to their administrators. There is a good deal of truth in the notion that America's schools are as good or as bad as the people want them to be.

In matters of internal policy like school discipline, the school boards turn freely to the advice of their administrators. They do not always heed this advice, especially when it conflicts with the expressed desires of powerful individuals or groups in the community, but for all practical purposes we can say that disciplinary policies are created by administrators and legalized by school boards. In many states the outlines of these policies are sharply contained by state laws and local customs, but there is usually a degree of freedom because communities vary considerably in the nature and number of disciplinary problems created by their youth.

The most frequent area of limitation by law is in the nature of punishment, but most of these laws, interpretations of laws, and customs are the results of pressures applied by well intentioned groups, sincere in their concern for the welfare of youth. It is usually possible to create effective policies even within these strait jackets.

The administrative team. In a small secondary school the administration of discipline is frequently a one-man operation, handled by the principal himself. There are many reasons for this and most of them are reasonable. To begin with, it is his *legal* responsibility. More important, it is his role by custom. This is his public image, the dispenser of justice, the symbol of authority. There is consistency in one-man rule if there is any consistency within the ruler. It can be consistently good or consistently bad, but consistent discipline is something which secondary school youngsters generally understand and accept.

When the school becomes larger, the principal often delegates this authority to an assistant. Now it becomes a two-man operation and consistency becomes a problem since no two men can view human failings identically. It also creates a very unpleasant job. Often a good classroom teacher is promoted out of the classroom to become custodian of this Pandora's box of misery. If he is very patient and very fair, he eventually will see his efforts rewarded. More and more he experiences the warm greetings of graduates he has helped in their adjustments to the world of regulations. The atmosphere of the school reflects his efforts. Teachers feel the added confidence of his backing. The fact remains, however, that not many men (rarely do women hold this particular job) remain content when their work is almost exclusively in the administration of discipline.

A more promising approach is a team venture in which the task is broken down and becomes a portion of the work of two or more people. Each school must find its own answer, but the real secret of success lies in a close and methodical co-ordination of all concerned. The principal cannot relinquish his share of the work no matter how large the school becomes.

We have referred to the various administrators as policy makers in respect to discipline. They usually do this by working out practical procedures for their particular schools. This process can be improved by putting the policies on paper for formal school board adoption, and we present a sample of such an actual policy statement.

Administrators may also create policies within their professional organizations. Each level of administration or specialty is usually represented by a regional, state, and national organization. It is entirely reasonable that these groups go on record on matters of school discipline. Everyone else seems to be getting into the act. Why not the ones closest to the problem every day? A written statement from a group of this stature on school discipline is usually newsworthy and can command favorable press attention.

The basic task of any disciplinarian from a total school point of view is to help the teacher and *to back him up.* Let us see how this works in practice.

The Vice-Principal (or the disciplinary officer with any official title) handles referrals from teachers of students who are interfering with the conduct of classes and who cannot be corrected in the classroom without stealing time from students who are ready to learn.

After receiving a written report from the teacher, the student is interviewed and admonished or punished on the basis of his total school record. Sometimes he may be referred to his guidance counselor, the school nurse, or some other specialist. Sometimes his parents are summoned for a conference. When the vice-principal has reached the end of his resources or when the violation is extremely serious, the student is referred directly to the principal.

The Principal studies the total picture. The case is discussed with the entire team, including the guidance director or the student's counselor before action is taken. Sometimes the student is granted another period of probation. Sometimes he is referred, with his parents, to the superintendent of schools.

The Superintendent may handle referrals of extreme cases in a manner similar to the principal. On occasion these go directly to the school board for action, especially if suspension is indicated.

The School Board, or subcommittee thereof, hears the case, with student, parents, and administrators present. Again, they may rule for another chance or they may suspend directly.

We emphasize that this is a *recommended* procedure and one which is being used in systems which have succeeded in setting a good disciplinary tone in their schools. It contrasts sharply with the usual procedure of leaving the entire problem up to the school principal and then failing to back him when the situation gets out of hand. The latter course is one of the important reasons why so many school systems have failed to maintain proper order in their secondary schools.

So we can see the dual function of the school administration in discipline; advising on or recommending policies, and acting as a channel of action in difficult cases. Both functions serve but one major purpose—helping the teacher in the classroom.

A WRITTEN DISCIPLINARY CODE

Every school has a code or philosophy of discipline. It may be merely a mirror image of the personality of the principal or of one of his stronger predecessors in office. It may be a hodgepodge of precedents and time-hazed recollections of precedents. It may be a semi-vacuum filled from time to time by the actions of a strong personality and imitations thereof. It may be, *and should be,* a carefully prepared written code of purpose and procedure reflecting a workable philosophy of education and the worthwhile values of the community.

The political structure of Great Britain rests on a complex foundation of concepts and precedents inherent in the experience of the people over many centuries. This great, free nation has no single guiding document as we have. American society bases its order on a great and living document, amazingly brief, which we know as the Constitution of the United States of America. What our forefathers considered to be the most worthy tenets of English free men were borrowed and put into new words with appropriate adaptations.

We can apply the same procedure to a school by preparing a statement of philosophy as a guide for its educational program. Similarly, we can codify the laws of the school by writing a disciplinary code. Some of the advantages of the process might be listed:

1. It focuses attention on positive moral values.
2. It makes discipline a working part of the school's philosophy of education.
3. It improves public relations.
4. It forces a reexamination of existing practices.
5. It can enhance the democratic aspects of school life by encouraging wider participation in policy making.
6. It formalizes procedures, making necessary adequate and methodical collection of data.
7. It clarifies every student's exact status.
8. It minimizes hasty and emotionally influenced action.
9. It establishes a clear-cut backing for teachers and administrators.
10. It increases efficiency of operation by eliminating duplication.

The nature of disciplinary codes will vary from community to community depending on laws, customs, specific problems of various areas, etc. Here is a sample code in use in a large, suburban high school in New England.

DISCIPLINARY CODE FOR __________ HIGH SCHOOL

__________ High School is a comprehensive high school dedicated to meeting the needs of all youth in its attendance area not better served by a more specialized institution. __________ High School students are served by competent teachers and administrators and a wide variety of specialists including a fulltime nurse, a special counselor coordinating community and state agency referrals, counselors for individual and group guidance, a speech therapist, a school psychologist, a school psychiatrist, a school physician, a placement teacher, and an attendance officer. While four of these specialists serve the entire school system, every student has access, without cost to all of these services.

__________ High School has a wide variety of offerings ranging from a sound and challenging college preparatory curriculum widely approved by the finest colleges to broad offerings and superior facilities in commercial preparation, home economics, art, music, machine shop, auto shop, wood shop, print shop, electronics lab, and vocational agriculture station as well as cooperative work experience programs in distributive education, medical secretarial work, and hospital aide training. We expect that any student who is willing to learn can find a profitable program within such a range of offerings.

Students who for various reasons are not willing to learn are given a great deal of time and attention by all of the specialists and administrators whose areas are applicable to the individual case. Failing in this, however, and after a number of parent conferences, if a student still refuses to cooperate and in so doing interferes with the opportunities of others, we feel that he should leave the school until such time as he is ready to profit from the program which has been provided at no little expense to the taxpayers. The first and paramount task of our school is to provide quality education for youngsters who are ready and willing to learn. We are not a psychiatric clinic nor a prison. We are a school.

These are the five steps of our procedure:

1. *The teacher* is expected to handle routine matters of discipline. When this interferes with his teaching, the student is sent to the appropriate disciplinary officer (Seniors to the Dean of Boys, Juniors to the Assistant Principal, Sophomores to the Administrative Assistant in charge of the Annex). The teacher need not concern himself with this division of responsibility when he sends a student out of the room. He simply sends him to the office.

It is expected that a written report follow sometime before the next day. Action will be taken on the basis of this report and the past record of the student. Teachers are invited to inquire about the disposition of the case, but cannot decide on punishment since they do not have the total picture of the student's school record. They are invited to confer and to recommend.

2. *The Disciplinary Officer* takes action based on the total record. In cases of frequent referral he sends a W.A.C. blank (report on work, attitude, conduct) to all of the student's teachers. On these he receives a complete and up-to-date report. He may then send the student home to return with his parents for a conference. This conference is treated as a total guidance conference and all data are brought together. It is not merely a discussion of the pupil's behavior problem. The Guidance Office is notified and, if appropriate to the case, the student's counselor is brought into the conference. In any event, the counselors are brought up to date at intervals on the disciplinary records of students and they have access to all W.A.C. reports which are filed in the student's confidential folder. If it becomes evident that the case should involve outside agencies, it is turned over to the Special Services Counselor who handles the case until it is settled, keeping in touch with the regular Counselor, the teachers, and the Disciplinary Officer.

In order to maintain close cooperation and consistency of action, all disciplinary officers meet with the Principal and the Guidance Director every Friday afternoon to review all cases handled during the week.

3. *The Principal* comes into the case when the Disciplinary Officer deems it advisable. The Principal then calls in the student and parents and reviews the entire record with them. Unless the current misbehavior is a flagrant defiance of authority calling for immediate referral to the Superintendent, the student is given another

opportunity to show improvement. If nothing else is heard from him within three weeks, the Principal sends for another set of W.A.C. reports from the teachers. If these reports show improvement, the student is summoned to the Principal's office for a conference in which he is praised for his efforts and urged to keep up the good work. His parents are also notified by telephone or letter of the improvement. If, on the other hand, the student has not improved, he is sent home. His parents are notified by letter that they are to call for an appointment with the Superintendent.

4. *The Superintendent* is presented with a complete record of the case and confers with the Principal or the Disciplinary Officer to clear up any questions which may arise.

Depending upon the case, the Superintendent places the student on probation or rules for immediate referral to the School Board (or subcommittee of same). As in the case of the Principal, follow up W.A.C. reports are sent to the Superintendent in three weeks in case of probation. If the student persists in poor behavior, he and his parents appear before the School Board or subcommittee.

5. *The School Board* reviews the entire case again, hears the student and his parents, questions the Superintendent and the Principal and takes one of two courses of action depending upon the record: (a) Probation (b) suspension for the remainder of the year.

In the case of suspension of a student under 16 years of age the entire history of the case is turned over to the Attendance Officer for referral to the Juvenile Court.

In this example of a disciplinary code, you will note that the school board becomes involved in a regular way, although the actual cases that will go that far will be very few. This is considered necessary in the state of Rhode Island where the illustration is in use, since only the school board (or school committee, as it is known in New England) has the power of suspension. In any event, the proponents of this procedure argue that if a school board is to be involved at all, it should be involved in a methodical way. When it deals with discipline in isolated, infrequent cases, it has no experience to draw from and is liable to take action that is inappropriately lenient or harsh. It is also true that a regular progression of steps has a profound effect on most young offenders, and an appearance before the school board is usually taken very seriously. Finally, school board participation is a logical climax to a teamwork process that starts with the classroom teacher.

11

Punishment as a Support for Discipline

In seeking a better understanding of the various theories of discipline as they exist in American classrooms today, a brief analysis of the history of discipline and punishment can be very illuminating. One interesting fact, for example, is that at many points in the history of education, school discipline has actually bordered on barbarism. This accounts, in part, for the many laws restricting methods of punishment in schools. Also to be found in history is the development of the legal basis of discipline as we know it today.

EVOLUTION OF THE AIMS AND METHODS OF DISCIPLINE

The change in concepts of discipline and punishment through the ages is tied to the dominant social and religious theories of an age. The most recent changes, for example, have resulted largely from our present awareness of democratic ideals and our rapidly increasing knowledge of mental health.

The development of the theories of discipline and, particularly, punishment may be roughly stated as follows:

1. Vindictive. The first theory for the treatment of bad behavior was vindictive. Revenge was the motif. Punishment was administered until the punisher was satisfied. There existed little thought of reforming the individual or of aiding him in achieving more acceptable behavior. The religious and social theories of most primitive peoples made this approach inevitable. Their belief in animism made them attribute motives to inanimate objects which were punished for injury to living persons. Their gods were vengeful and despotic. Even the Jehovah of the Old Testament was a wrathful God.

2. Retributive. A step beyond mere revenge was the adoption of the retributive theory. The belief was that if one does evil he must suffer fitting consequences. The basis of this conception can be found in natural law, but its origin is likely to be found in the emergence of better ethical and religious ideology. Now the gods or a God would give people rules by which to live. The codes of Hammurabi and of Moses illustrate this concept, and they had tremendous influence in shaping human thought.

3. Deterrent. The deterrent theory had fear as its basis even to a greater degree than the earlier theories. The religious doctrines associated with this theory are well known. The individual was considered to be inherently evil because of "original sin," and could be deterred from crime by the example of unpleasant punishment. As a result, public executions were common, and in the classroom children were either beaten publicly or held up to ridicule if they misbehaved.

4. Remedial. The remedial theory is fairly recent in origin and is based on an increasing knowledge resulting from research into the nature of human personality. The weakening of the previous type of religious thought has contributed considerably to its development. Behavior is considered to be an outgrowth of the total life history of the individual, and diagnosis and cure are the desired processes. The aim of this theory is to restore the individual to socially acceptable behavior patterns.

5. Preventive. The preventive theory is the natural outgrowth of the social thinking and research of the modern era. Its aim is to prevent the situations which call for remedial measures. An enormous amount of anti-social behavior would never occur if we could remove its causes and provide a desirable environment in which children could grow. An effective curriculum adapted to individual differences, well trained and competent teachers, adequate materials, and desirable physical facilities are regarded as essential in securing good discipline. The aim of the school is to produce an individual possessed of a social conscience who sees the good sense in acceptable behavior. This is basic to a democratic society.

THE LEGAL BASIS OF DISCIPLINE

Legally the teacher stands *in loco parentis* in respect to pupil control since by sending a child to school, the parents delegate to the teacher authority to discipline the pupil for all offenses which interfere with the good order and effective control of the school. The teacher, however, is restricted to the limits of his jurisdiction and responsibilities *as a teacher.* Jurisdiction extends to all offenses committed against the authority of the school within its legal limitations and school regulations, whether the offenses occur on or off the school grounds, and before, during, or after school hours. This is true to an appreciable extent in every state and territory of the United States.

Corporal punishment. There is a great deal of current controversy over corporal punishment, and there seems to be a growing trend throughout the country to regard a return to its use in our school systems as a partial answer to the problems of delinquency. While only the District of Columbia and the State of New Jersey specifically prohibit corporal punishment by statute, a Rhode Island law may be similarly interpreted, although corporal punishment is not specifically mentioned.

The school laws of Rhode Island regarding suspension are stated as follows:

> The School Committee may suspend during pleasure all pupils found guilty of corrigibly bad conduct or of violation of the school regulation.
>
> *Note:* It is generally held to be law that a school committee or board of education may not exclude a pupil for a period longer than the current school year.
>
> *Note:* The state statutes are silent on the matter of corporal punishment of pupils. The subject is usually governed by rule of the school committee.

The basic idea of Horace Mann was to replace authoritarianism and corporal punishment by strengthening and improving the ability and the quality of the teacher. Much has been written for and against corporal punishment, but only a brief summary of the writings on this subject will be presented here.

Since 1833, about 59 cases have been brought against teachers as a result of corporal punishment. Almost all of these cases were for assault and battery. Most courts decided in favor of the teacher under the common law rule that he stands *in loco parentis,* that the punishment was justified by the behavior of the pupil, and that it was not unreasonable, excessive, or malicious.

The following actions were considered to be excessive or malicious:

Teacher beat, bruised, cut, and gashed a pupil's head. (1953)

Principal dragged a ten-year-old pupil to floor and sat and knelt on pupil, exerting weight on pupil's abdomen. (1954)

Principal and teacher severely beat a twelve-year-old pupil. (1954)

These cases show that the courts will quickly condemn unreasonable and cruel punishment. Teachers and courts agree that corporal punishment, when administered, should be administered reasonably. Some students with emotional and/or behavioral problems do not respond to the counseling of the school or to less severe types of punishment. Quite often the problem youngster must undergo rapid improvement if he is to remain at school at all, and we cannot escape from the fact that some pupils do show a favorable change in their overt behavior after corporal punishment is administered.

One significant fact was made apparent by the court's action in the case of *The State vs. Lutz* and that was that "a teacher is more impersonal in punishment than a parent who might punish because of ill feeling toward close relatives."

Under the common law of *in loco parentis* a teacher may act only to a certain extent. He is not versed with all the rights, duties, and responsibilities of parents. His authority extends only to those aspects of child behavior which have an effect upon or are related to the teacher's performance of his professional duties. A teacher is not a free agent to punish a child to any extent and in any manner that suits his fancy.

The decision to resort to corporal punishment is an administrative one. Before the decision is made many facts must be considered. No decision should be made without considerable knowledge of the student as well as of his offense. The consensus of opinion throughout the country may well be summed up by the words of a rural Ohio superintendent who said that in 33 years in the business he had never had to whip a youngster but that he didn't want to take the privilege away from any teacher who felt there was no other way to handle a specific situation.

We question seriously the effectiveness of corporal punishment in the secondary grades. On the other hand, we do not feel that this matter should be settled by law on any but the local level and then only by school board action. State laws prohibiting corporal punishment are largely anachronistic. They can be used for dubious purposes by certain scheming students and they are, in a real sense, an insult to a noble profession. Their very existence implies a lack of confidence in our teachers.

Numerous studies indicate that a majority of superintendents are in favor of some form of corporal punishment. Professional educators reached by questionnaires are also in favor of the punishment being carried out by an administrator. The use of some type of suspension in secondary schools rather than corporal punishment is clearly indicated.

THE IMPORTANCE OF PRINCIPLES IN DISCIPLINE

The importance of the individual teacher's understanding of certain principles underlying modern school discipline cannot be overstated. If the teacher understands and accepts a sound statement of principles and *applies* this philosophy in his daily classroom routine, the result should be methods which secure effective and gratifying results.

Let us consider briefly some principles applicable to secondary school discipline. One may draw from many excellent statements of this sort by writers in the field, but we find that most of them are heavily influenced by theory. Since it is our purpose to combine the theoretical with a heavy emphasis on the practical, we offer the following:

PRINCIPLES OF SECONDARY SCHOOL DISCIPLINE

1. Disciplinary policies should be in harmony with the total goals of education. The disciplinary procedures of a school should never be permitted to become an end in themselves, nor to be confused with procedures necessary in other types of institutions. The first criterion for any secondary school disci-

plinary procedure should be the question, "Is this a sound *educational* practice?"

2. Disciplinary policies should be in harmony with the teachings of science; notably psychology and sociology.

3. Disciplinary policies should be in harmony with the principles of a democratic society, i.e. equal justice for all, respect for the rights and dignity of the individual, humanitarian treatment for all.

4. Disciplinary policies should stress the *responsibilities* as well as the rights of an individual.

5. Disciplinary policies should be positive and directed to the goal of *self discipline.* The emphasis should be on the benefits to the group and to the individual of good self discipline rather than on punitive measures.

6. Disciplinary policies should be primarily preventive, secondarily corrective, and never retributive.

REWARDS AND PUNISHMENT

The daily use of rewards and punishment by the classroom teacher presents an opportunity for an examination of their values in attaining the goal of self discipline within the pupils. When a person accomplishes something which is significant to him, he derives much more satisfaction from the achievement itself than from any possible extrinsic reward. This becomes increasingly apparent as a student matures. Therefore, in the classroom, particularly in the secondary school, the student should expect no prize for conducting himself appropriately in the furtherance of a significant school enterprise; however, in most instances for good conduct he would be likely to receive the recognition, approval, and encouragement of his teacher and fellow students. The most gratifying and educative recognition of superior conduct is the granting of more freedom and responsibility to the individual pupil. Instead of giving the child an extrinsic reward, the result is intrinsic and presents a new incentive to further growth. More importantly it is a reward which is available to every child.

Sound educational rewards are those: (1) which have no value in themselves, (2) which open the way to greater opportunities for service to the group, (3) which are within reach of every member of the group, (4) which are granted to all who reach the standard previously set, and (5) which are selected or accepted by the group.

The question now arises as to when the teacher must resort to punishment and what type of punishment should be used for a particular offense under particular circumstances. The teacher bases his decision on the theory of discipline which he has accepted and on the principles involved.

TYPES OF PUNISHMENT IN COMMON USE

We pointed out in the preface that America's thousands of school districts are not characterized by extreme diversity; on the contrary, many things are done in the same way in many places. Part of the reason for this is that we share a more or less common heritage, and part of that is a strong tendency to do things that get *results.* So it is with punitive measures in our secondary schools. With the exception of certain schools which by their very nature deviate from the norm, most American secondary schools employ disciplinary policies which fall into a fairly regular pattern. Let us examine briefly some of these common practices used by teachers and administrators.

It is generally agreed by school administrators that teachers should be responsible for discipline in their own classrooms. This means that most punishment is administered by teachers, albeit the most serious punishment is administered by administrators. Under certain conditions it becomes necessary for the teacher to refer a student to the office. Examples of this would be:

1. When the teacher has lost control and cannot regain it without help. (This happens now and then even to thoroughly competent teachers, under unusual circumstances.)

2. When the disturbance stems from a cause which requires special attention such as a mental disturbance.

3. When the teacher feels that a student must be removed temporarily from the class. In this case he may prefer to deal with the case himself at a later time and will indicate this by note or telephone call to the office. In any case where a student is sent to the office a message should follow immediately. A student who is temporarily disturbed should not be permitted to wander.

4. When the teacher has exhausted his resources and feels that the case must be turned over to the administration. In this event the teacher should feel that decision as to punishment must also be referred. The principal or his deputy must now assign punishment in terms of the student's total school record and should not be expected to avenge the teacher's injured feelings. It is reasonable to expect that a recommendation from the teacher be considered, but with the referral of the problem should go the referral of judgment. Otherwise the principal's role would be merely that of executioner. Contrary to what a few teachers may think, this is not his main task!

What, then, are the methods to which the teacher may turn for punishment, when inner controls seems to have failed, and when the student's behavior pattern interferes with the learning opportunities of other students? Corporal punishment has already been discussed. Generally it should be dismissed as a weapon in the secondary school teacher's arsenal.

The reprimand. The most common device and the one most frequently resorted to as a first choice is the reprimand. If administered calmly and without the heat of anger it can be very effective even when used publicly. As a rule, however, it should be reserved for private use and certainly severe reprimands should not be public spectacles. Indeed, these sometimes have an effect just the opposite of the teacher's intent. For some students a public reprimand is considered to be most desirable. It gives them the spotlight of attention and, they feel, it raises their status with their fellow students. This is substantially true if the teacher is considered to be unfair or "grouchy." In this case sharp reprimands actually increase the incentive to misbehave and thus create a vicious circle which can only end with a pronounced change of attitude and approach on the part of the teacher.

The conference. Strictly speaking, the pupil-teacher conference should not be listed as a punishment device, but we must admit that it can have overtones of punishment when it is held after school as a result of misbehavior. For one thing, the pupil is forced to remain after school for the appointment. This can be a very real punishment in itself if the student works after school or if he takes a bus home. In junior high grades or in cases where students are bused from long distances over roads not serviced by public transportation, the school may have a policy which does not permit detention after school for any purpose. In most cases high school students should be expected to remain after school for any number of reasons with the understanding that a one day deferment may be granted in order to arrange transportation or to make adjustments with an employer.

The conference can be a most effective means of getting to the bottom of misbehavior. If the teacher wishes the conference to be more than a prolonged reprimand, he should take steps to set a positive, goal-centered tone. A good starting point might be the student's vocational plans. From this the teacher could work quickly back to the need for graduation from high school and the importance of passing *this course.* Once teacher and student have reached a genuine agreement on this much, the rest should follow rather easily. If the student cannot agree to these points, a referral to Guidance is clearly indicated. The discussion may relax into a friendly chat, but the summary by the teacher should review the student's exact status at this point. Threats are usually unnecessary but the student should understand fully what steps he may force the teacher to take next if his behavior continues unchanged. The student should leave the conference with the conviction that the teacher has offered help.

Detention. Another popular device, as old as education itself, and one which has met with court approval, is "staying after school." Opinions vary on this practice and many schools have abandoned it completely. Other schools are firm in retaining it and one may conclude that if detention is to be used as a punitive device, certain safeguards must be observed.

When detention is used for punishment rather than as enforced academic assistance, it is most effective as a means of annoying the annoyer. There is a certain crude justice in retaining the student who continually fails to return his report card or constantly comes to class without his pencil and/or books. Then there is the student who is habitually tardy to class or to school for flimsy reasons. Most teachers and parents can readily see the appropriateness of this type of punishment for these offenses.

Detention cannot be successfully extended to serious offenses. While one hour of detention may be entirely appropriate for "cutting" one class, it does not follow that five hours is an appropriate punishment for a day of truancy because five classes are "cut." Disciplinary policies do not lend themselves to such neat mathematical precision. Truancy is not merely an extension of cutting one class—it is a more disturbing symptom and one that should be treated in a different manner. Detention, if used at all, has its limitations even in minor offenses and cannot be multiplied for application to more serious misbehavior.

The fallacy that it can probably stems from an imitation of the now largely discredited practice of attaching to certain crimes so many years of imprisonment.

One very practical reason for limiting assignments of detention is the "lifer" attitude. When a student is faced with an accumulation of fifteen or twenty hours it merely means that, for him, school is an hour longer. He no longer fears further detention. He now begins to think like the prisoner who is serving a life sentence without hope of parole in a state which outlaws capital punishment. What can be done to him now?

Detention should not be permitted to sink to the level of sitting. Some students do far too much of this in school as it is. Each student should be required to have study materials with him, and silence should be strictly enforced. (The detention room, study halls, and the library are three places where old fashioned pin-drop silence should still be evident.) We know, of course, that this will not ensure that every student will accomplish any real work, but it will provide an opportunity for those who want it. One principal who enforces this type of detention swears that many students *like* to be assigned there because it guarantees them an hour of uninterrupted work—something they cannot find at home. One can easily argue that the school should provide facilities of this sort without confusing them with punishment. Teachers wonder how many would seek them out. With the detention assignment is included the essential factor of *enforcement.* To many an adolescent this is still badly needed. We can look to the horizon for the happy day when our schools will be so effective that built-in motivation will be adequate. In the meantime we must work with conditions as they are. We do not propose to pursue this point because we consider the detention device to be a straw man who can easily be knocked into the dust. If a school wants to use it, it might as well provide the opportunity for purposeful study.

Enforced labor. The student who has written his priceless witticisms on the basement wall can usually see the justice in being required to wash the entire wall. The student who has defaced school property faces philosophically the punishment of repairing the damage he has done. This punishment has wide acceptance as being appropriate and fair if administered wisely. The temptation is sometimes great when a culprit has been caught in the act, to assign excessive penalties of this nature. One recalls from former years such choice military punishments as scrubbing a drill hall floor with a tooth brush. This may or may not have been effective then and there, but it has no place in a modern secondary school. Serious vandalism, like repeated truancy, is a disturbing symptom, and cannot be treated by an extended use of this popular device. It should be referred for appropriate treatment.

Fines. Just as fines are regarded as appropriate for certain adult offenses, they are sometimes used in schools. Librarians seem to find them essential for maintaining control of the equitable use of books. Damaged school property must be replaced or repaired by the taxpayers. It is entirely fitting that the guilty party should pay if he cannot repair the damage. You will note that we say guilty person, not the parents of the guilty person. Here, again, certain safeguards are in order. Steps should be taken, by letter or by conference, to see that the student does not simply obtain the money from his parents. He should *work* for the money either by cleaning the cellar for his parents or by working at a part-time job. For the student whose parents are without adequate income there should be an opportunity to work around the school. He can then be paid from a special fund in order to pay his fine or the fine can be written off in exchange for the work. This differs from enforced labor as described above in that the work does not necessarily have to be appropriate to the nature of the offense.

It should also be pointed out that the courts have not looked with favor upon fining students without an alternative punishment such as the legendary "Ten dollars or ten days." The principal who excludes a pupil for failure to pay a fine and for which no alternative is offered, is on dubious ground if the matter goes to court.

Loss of privileges. Another popular punishment which also seems most appropriate from time to time is loss of privileges. In some high schools seniors are granted certain privileges which cannot be extended to the entire student body. Abuse of these privileges can very justly be punished by loss of same. A great deal depends on interpretation. Common sense and good judgment would not permit hasty and arbitrary withdrawal of privileges for petty reasons. These privileges are taken seriously by most students, and their loss is a serious matter to them.

Isolation in the classroom. This is probably a more fitting device for the lower elementary school than for the secondary school, but it is sometimes used by teachers who feel that a childish punishment should attend a childish offense. Like the use of sarcasm, this weapon should be labelled "handle with care." Subjection of a student to ridicule has been largely rejected as a dangerous practice in modern schools. This is not to say, of course, that the teacher should avoid utilizing her seating arrangements as preventive medicine. Like the chairman of a meeting who is well acquainted with the participants, the teacher can prevent a great deal of annoyance by judicious seating arrangements.

Suspension from class. It sometimes becomes necessary to exclude a student from class for more than one day, but this usually requires the consent and cooperation of the administration. If a student has been extremely rude, for example, this action might be justified for a few days. In this way he is not denied the opportunities of the other classes where, presumably, he has not offended anyone. Yet, he is faced with the seriousness of his offense. This should be regarded as a fairly drastic punishment since it involves a definite academic penalty.

Expulsion from class. Permanent exclusion from class should not generally be used as punishment in academic classes. Offenses grave enough to warrant this punishment probably deserve completely different treatment such as suspension from school. In certain types of classes, however, such as shops, the element of physical danger should be carefully weighed. If a student persists in behavior which might lead to injury for himself or for other students, he should be excluded from the class until he demonstrates a radical shift in attitude. Immaturity does not usually end overnight so this probably would mean the deferment of this particular opportunity for another year.

Teachers in shops where dangers exist (and dangers exist wherever there are sharp tools) should have the complete cooperation and backing of the administration. If their judgment is sound enough to be entrusted with a class, it is sound enough to follow in a recommendation of exclusion for reasons of safety. Theirs is a very special responsibility and worthy of very special consideration. A band saw can cause far more physical damage than a Latin book.

"Mikado" punishments. Some teachers are talented in creating punishments that fit the crime, sometimes quite effectively and amusingly. One biology teacher in a large suburban high school kept a supply of pencils carefully shortened so that they could be used only with considerable annoyance to the user. These he loaned to students who "forgot" their pencils. Several generations of students may have forgotten a great many things about their high school days, but they seldom forgot his pencil stubs. Devices like this can be harmless if they do not expose students to sharp ridicule, and they sometimes add a bit of spice to school life.

Demerits. Demerit systems are popular at military schools. Students are assessed so many demerits for various minor offenses and must "work them off" in various unpleasant ways. These systems are sometimes useful but they involve a good deal of petty bookkeeping. A teacher may wish to try a variation on this theme in his own room. If so, he should involve the students in the planning so that it does not become an object of ridicule. Usually this device is not applicable in public schools.

Forced withdrawal from school. The terms *suspension, expulsion,* and *exclusion* are often used erroneously and interchangeably. A study of court actions reveals that there is general agreement on the following: (1) *suspension* is usually temporary, (2) *expulsion* is permanent, or for a substantial length of time, (3) the power to suspend or expel undoubtedly rests with the school board except where state laws specify otherwise (as in Rhode Island) and when the device is used reasonably as a last resort. Other terms such as *exclusion* have become popular recently, possibly out of a desire to avoid legal technicalities. Such subterfuge is probably pointless, however, since the courts would interpret the act as suspension or expulsion under the general definitions listed above.

Suspension from school is usually an administrative penalty and is not imposed by a teacher. It should be considered as a last resort and used sparingly. When the principal feels that it is the only way of protecting the group from depraved or dangerous influence, he should not hesitate to suspend. Similarly, when the offense is shocking to an extreme, immediate suspension is essential. The Superintendent, and probably the School Board will have to be involved in cases of this sort.

Ordinarily, however, two methods which are sometimes erroneously called suspension, may be used. First, there is the practice of sending a student home with instructions that he may return if accompanied by a parent. This serves the dual purpose of enforcing a parent conference and of underscoring the seriousness of the offense. The disadvantage is that the parent usually arrives with a chip on his shoulder, primed only with the student's side of the story. The skillful administrator can usually overcome this by first letting the parent "blow off steam" and then by calmly steering the conference through the facts of the immediate situation to a full consideration of the total picture. The emphasis should be on the student's goals and how home and school can work together to help him achieve them. This practice can be extremely effective when all ordinary means of communication with parents have failed. At the time of the interview, the principal should have all the student's records before him, including complete and recent reports from every teacher concerned.

The other variation on the suspension idea is called into play when a student obviously does not belong in school at that particular time. He may have run the gamut of appeal and counseling and nothing has seemed to work. He may look upon school as a lark. If he is over 16 at this point, a parting of the ways until the next school year can often be very beneficial, especially if he tries his hand at a fulltime job in the interim. It is presumptuous of us to assume that we have all the answers to all the problems of all students within the walls of our schools.

If the parents cannot see the wisdom of such a step, the principal can point out that the alternative may be a formal suspension which carries with it an entry in the permanent record. Voluntary withdrawal can be listed there and will not affect adversely future recommendations. Perhaps this can be viewed as a polite form of blackmail, but many principals feel that it works wonders. Their experience is that many of these students return to school with an improved attitude.

These, then, are some of the more common punitive measures

used in our secondary schools. Many teachers and administrators feel that they work. Where they do work, it is usually because they are administered with mature judgment and a good deal of common sense.

12

The School and Delinquency

The familiar line of yellow buses, bumper to bumper in the loading circle, awaited the daily invasion as dismissal time drew near. Across the street a few dutiful mother-chauffeurs sat in their station wagons, and here and there a battered convertible with an impatient boy friend in the saddle breathed blue smoke out of dual exhausts. Suddenly an outside bell jangled and moments later the building erupted buoyant high schoolers from every exit. In less than a minute the streets and sidewalks were filled with happy kids, full of plans for the afternoon and spilling over with laughter and chatter.

To the casual observer there would be a remarkable sameness about these youngsters—about the way they talked, acted, and dressed, a studied homogeneity. But if the same observer strolled a block down the street and paused for a moment in front of the corner variety store his eye would immediately catch the difference in the four boys clustered there.

These, too, were like each other but different—sharply different—from all the others. Each wore his hair long in the careful carelessness of the "DA" haircut—effeminate in a decadent way and in strange contrast to the total effect of theatrical and aggressive masculinity—black leather jackets, dirty jeans, and dull black motorcycle boots.

Here was the prototype of the juvenile delinquent as Hollywood might have portrayed him—dangling cigarette butt, carefully cultivated slouch, and defiance written into every gesture. The four boys talked, laughed, pushed each other playfully, and punctuated their muttered obscenities with frequent spitting on the sidewalk. The few girls who were rash enough or naive enough to pass before them got the full treatment. Most of the boys seemed to prefer the other side of the street.

Shorn of their uniforms and haircuts, these four would look very much like all the other boys. Their insides were perhaps tight with longing as they insulted the girls and their hearts undoubtedly yearned for companionship as they sneered at the boys. They spoke scornfully of the school they no longer attended, yet they seemed to do a good deal of their lounging in its vicinity. It seemed as if their carefully affected clothing and mannerisms were trying to say to the world, "Look at us. We belong. We amount to something. We dress this way because we know it offends you!"

So much has been written about delinquent youth that it seems superfluous to add anything, and yet the school cannot sweep this social crisis under a convenient rug. It must understand the problem and attempt to deal with it within the limitations of its facilities and its basic mission to provide education for all youth who are willing to accept it.

It would be simpler to assume that the four youths described above live in a different world from that of the youngsters on their way home from school, but they do not. It is true that they have travelled the entire route of classroom misbehavior, truancy, and maladjustment onto their street corner and into their uniforms of rebellion, but many of the youngsters still enrolled in the school are travelling the same road. The difference is a matter of degree, and the school can do several things to halt or to slacken the process.

Most delinquents have gone wrong not because of a real desire to be bad, but because of a driving force within them that demands expression. The normal youngster may possess the same force, but to a lesser degree. In spite of emotionally disturbed homes, in spite of unfavorable surroundings, only a small percentage of our youth become actively delinquent. Some of these are born with an emotional predisposition to aggressive behavior, and under certain conditions they will surely drift into delinquency, but if given a favorable environment, their energies can be constructively channelled.

As it affects, and is affected by juvenile delinquency, the school cannot escape an awareness of its responsibility, its strategic advantages, and the fact that the community expects it to do something to help solve this perplexing problem.

THE SCHOOL'S RESPONSIBILITIES

There are, as we have pointed out, definite limits to the school's responsibilities. It is primarily an educational institution and not a social agency nor a psychiatric clinic. Within these limits, however, the school has certain functions which it has always accepted and which bear directly on the problem of reclaiming wayward youth.

The community's attitude. In its concern and bewilderment over delinquency, the community is turning anxiously to all of its agencies for action. Its attitude toward the school might be summarized as follows:

1. *The secondary school has a mandate to provide education for* all *American youth not better served by other types of institutions.* This includes wayward youth, and if a more suitable institution is unavailable or inadequate, the school should try to fill the gap. This attitude conflicts with the school's usual

understanding of its function and knowledge of its limitations. It usually goes without saying that this service is expected at no extra cost.

The school has only three choices of action in response to this demand. It can simply ignore the whole proposition and continue business as usual. It can outline a program of action, including a request for additional facilities and specialized personnel, and ask the people to foot the bill; an approach which has met with some success in certain junior high schools serving sensitive areas of New York City. Or it can attempt to step up its guidance and referral services, and try to effect a closer cooperation with existing agencies without a sharp increase in cost and without injuring the quality of its educational program. In spite of the fact that many administrators would denounce it as impossible, the last course of action may be the most sensible for most communities since schools do not usually pretend to have definitive answers to this world-wide problem, and have no desire to deal in quackery.

2. *The school represents the desirable values of society and is charged with the responsibility of passing these values on to the young.* There can be little argument here except to say that the school cannot do this job without the assistance of the entire community. If the community places a premium on fun and games, makes a fetish of "adjustment," and is reluctant to say NO to pampered youth, the schools inevitably deteriorate into pleasure palaces in spite of the good intentions and serious efforts of the educators. A good deal of magazine space has exposed this particular illness in certain regions of our country to the dismay of educators elsewhere.

The World War II years, and the decade following the war, saw perceptible decay in values and a tremendous increase in materialistic thinking. The possession of gadgets has become a major national goal aided, no doubt by the fantastic selling power of television. Today's delinquent is a product of this environment. He does not reject the false values of society—he takes them to his heart. He wants all these things, and simply rejects the idea of working for them. An automobile of his own is not a desirable luxury to him—it is, in his opinion, his *right!* When he cannot have one, he may steal it. Of course the school can fight against this outrageous line of thinking, but if it must fight alone the battle will be lost.

3. *The school is staffed with trained personnel specifically equipped to work with youth.* This is true, especially in the better school systems, but there is still the annoying and persistent question of how far the school is expected to wander from its basic tasks. If the people want the schools to become treatment agencies for unbalanced youngsters, they must make their school boards aware of this, effect a change of policy, and be prepared to implement their desires with adequate financial support. A guidance counselor can handle a good many students if most of them are normal and if those with serious problems represent only a small percentage of his case load. When the number of difficult cases increases, the normal students are neglected. One might be willing to make this sacrifice if the counselor manages to make appreciable inroads into the very serious cases. It is not our opinion that he can. By the time he sees them it is usually too late for anything he can do.

4. *The school offers opportunities for association with normal youngsters.* This is frequently cited by parole officers who wish to have their charges reinstated in school. The principal realizes the importance of these associations, but he is also aware of his responsibility to protect his normal students from dangerous influences. A good deal depends upon the attitude of the delinquent. If he has become too hardened and twisted he will get no benefit from associating with other youngsters and he can do a great deal of harm to them.

5. *The school is partly to blame for delinquency and should, therefore, do something about combatting it.* There is little

doubt that inadequacies of the school, notably the lack of a curriculum with real meaning for a segment of our youth, have contributed to the problem. Perhaps the errors of the school in this respect are of omission rather than of commission and the school has failed to prevent some delinquency. It is rather absurd to take the position that even our poorer schools have created delinquency. But be that as it may, we can hope that the considerable improvements in the quality of public education since World War II will tend eventually to cut down the size of the problem. There is little disagreement as to the role of the school in the prevention of delinquency. Differences exist mainly as to how much correction may be expected.

Delinquency and school goals. Precedents for extensive efforts in the battle against delinquency may be found in at least three historic goals of American schools:

(1) *American schools have always been charged with the responsibility of building and strengthening democracy.* The growth of delinquency is a serious threat to democracy and to our nation. While it is difficult to pinpoint the exact extent of delinquency due to a lack of uniformity in record keeping, there is little doubt that the incidence of delinquency has been steadily increasing since World War II.

We have ample evidence that youth delinquency is not confined to America. The "Teddy boys" of London, the hooligans of various Russian cities, and the bored thrill seekers of Stockholm, have all received their share of newspaper space. A democracy is more dependent on the quality of its citizenship than a totalitarian nation since the will of the people or the apathy of the people is more directly reflected in the quality of its leaders. The totalitarian nations are much more purposeful in taking over the direction of their schools to use them for their own ends. In democratic nations the schools reflect more directly the society in which they exist, but there seems to be little direction and organization toward the goal of *using* the schools to further the goals of democracy.

We must overcome our fear of highly colored words such as *propaganda* and *brainwashing* and recognize the fact that organized indoctrination is essential to habit formation and especially vital in the correction of poor habits and attitudes. It need not follow that this indoctrination must be poisoned by the narrow doctrines we seem to flirt with in times of crisis. The central theme can continue to be a simple and firm belief in a way of life that recognizes the dignity of the individual, and we should hammer home the message that young people must accept the responsibilities as well as the rights of citizenship. There is nothing essentially fixed or narrow in this theme—it can include all manner of change and flexibility as long as it remains within the framework of the great, ongoing purposes of democracy.

One small, rural high school experimented with a series of short assembly programs which preached rather directly about the values of a democratic society and the responsibilities of the individual therein. The following year a lengthy and anonymous questionnaire was administered to the entire student body. The questionnaire was very broad and tested only indirectly the attitudes stressed in the assembly programs. The results were very gratifying. The students seemed to have soaked up the desirable attitudes and expressed them as their own. Whether or not they retained them or applied them is, of course, open to conjecture, but the school felt that it had done *something,* and that something was better than nothing!

In spite of the haphazard way in which we seem to develop citizenship in our schools, most secondary school administrators take an optimistic view of this task because they have seen so many of their poorest school citizens mature into useful members of society once they have been thrust into the responsibilities of adulthood. The pertinent question is whether these people become good citizens *because* of the school or *in spite of* the school.

(2) *American schools have always been expected to work toward the goal of equality of opportunity.* That they have failed to achieve it has been largely due to matters beyond their control such as local prejudices, general apathy, and wide differences of communities in ability and willingness to pay for education.

In recent years equality of opportunity has taken on a new interpretation. Where formerly it meant an equal chance to benefit from a single basic curriculum, it now means the provision of a fitting curriculum for each child according to his aspirations and abilities. While this viewpoint has received more attention in print than in practice, it is no mean achievement to have reached general agreement in principle on this issue. Practice will surely follow and with it will come a decline in the percentage of wayward youth.

(3) *American schools have generally been deeply concerned with the discovery and development of talent.* Talent should be sought out, not merely because the world and our nation need it—but simply because it exists, and it sometimes appears in near-delinquents or in delinquents. Gang leaders frequently possess many talents. Weak and inadequate youngsters are drawn into delinquency by the personal magnetism of some of these leaders who seem to have all the qualities admired by the less able youth around them. To their followers, gang leaders are modern Robin Hoods. To society, they are just ordinary hoods. To the schools, they should be key individuals who must be redirected for their own sakes and for the sakes of their followers.

A suburban high school developed a leadership program which offered certain opportunities for direct and effective participation in civic affairs. A conscious effort was made to involve youngsters with leadership potential who seemed to be moving in the wrong direction. While it has not been felt that this program alone has prevented delinquency, it has been noted in a few dramatic instances that youngsters involved have inproved in their academic work and have gone on to colleges and technical institutions. The program certainly did not hurt them, and it did expose them to direct contact with more desirable youngsters who otherwise would certainly have shunned them.

THE SCHOOL'S LIMITATIONS

The secondary school faces a perpetual dilemma in respect to juvenile delinquency. It is usually poorly equipped to deal with severe cases, and it must protect the majority of its students against the evil influence of the minority. Yet it must recognize its responsibility as an important bulwark of defense against a disease that seriously threatens our society. It looks for an answer in trying to do what it can within its limitations, somewhat in the manner of the general practitioner of medicine whose professional honesty and discretion compel him to refer occasional patients to specialists.

It is difficult to draw a sharp line of distinction between those causers of serious disciplinary problems in school who may yet be saved, and the delinquents who must be referred to another agency or simply removed from the school. The symptoms are very similar in kind, differing only in degree, but the qualified school principal learns by experience to recognize the peculiar combination of signs which can only lead to exclusion and/or referral:

1. Continued and universal lack of application in most or all subjects. This, in itself, is considered just cause for suspension in many schools.
2. General agreement among a student's teachers that they can do nothing for him.

3. Continued and obvious bad influence. Sometimes the presence of an individual in a class changes the entire behavior pattern of the class. Students seem to misbehave to seek the approval of the maladjusted one. When he is removed, the class resumes its normal behavior. It is extremely difficult to convince a teacher that there is any justification for retaining a person of this sort.

4. Continued and frequent truancy.

5. Inability of the counselor to communicate because of cynicism or lack of responsiveness of the student. This is, perhaps, the most serious symptom of all. If the counselor cannot reach the individual and establish a working relationship, the school has very likely exhausted its resources. The counselor must learn to distinguish between genuine and lip-service co-operation. The delinquent often attempts to "con" his counselor into a sympathetic attitude in order to remain in school for reasons of his own which usually have nothing in common with the purposes of the school.

6. Constant evasiveness and lying. When a youth seeks refuge in a world of fantasy, he becomes a very skillful liar, often to the point of convincing himself that he is telling the truth.

7. Extreme and obvious symptoms of mental disorder.

8. An abnormal preoccupation with sex. Teachers become quickly aware of the student who constantly uses filthy language even when he thinks he cannot be heard. Parents are extremely fearful of this influence on their children and expect the school officials to eliminate it from the school.

A PROGRAM OF ACTION TO HELP DROPOUTS

Perhaps a first consideration of the school should be the process of separation itself. When a student drops out or is dropped from school, the responsibility of the school should not cease abruptly at the door. This is a very crucial point in the life of the youngster and a reasonable attempt should be made to follow up his progress for at least a year or two. The mere evidence that someone is interested in him may prevent a wasted life.

Follow-up presupposes some cooperation on the part of the youth, of course. Failing in this, the school can seek some avenue of referral, for this youngster is like a live wire dangling from a pole. Unless skilled attention is available soon, someone may get hurt. If a parole officer is involved he should be alerted immediately. The youth's parents, his clergyman, a social worker, a counselor in the United States Employment Service, an experienced recruiting sergeant, a juvenile division police officer, or the Judge of the Juvenile Court may prove helpful. All professional youth workers recognize the advantages of preventive action at strategic moments.

If the youngster is cooperative to some degree, the school can use its placement service to help him find a suitable job. In this case the prospective employer should be notified of the facts in the case. Many employers are perfectly willing to take a risk to save a youngster. If the employer does not understand the circumstances, he may discharge the youth without giving him a reasonable chance, thus compounding the maladjustment. Even in the school without a placement service, the principal usually has contacts in his circle of friends who would be willing to help a youth like this. The prevention of delinquency must become *everybody's* business.

Moving back to the period before the exclusion or drop-out, the larger school can group these young people for intensive employment orientation. Why worry about taking them out of classes which have become meaningless for them? They may even be able to bridge the gap between school and work by a process of part-time employment. Indeed, a part-time job is often a means of holding a youngster in school. The experience of some financial independence has provided the needed miracle in many cases. This is amply demonstrated in the schools having successful work-experience programs. While it is perfectly true that the active delinquent is a poor risk for such a program, many pre-delinquents have made remarkable adjustments through such plans.

The counselor should take the responsibility for follow-up. Some counselors enjoy this work and do it very well. Pre-delinquents should be assigned to them as soon as they are identified. Sometimes the administrator responsible for discipline can carry out these duties. This is very logical since it adds a positive facet to what can become a fairly negative job. It also enhances his prestige with the problem cases since they learn very quickly that his function is to help them, not merely to administer punishment.

In the general area of treating pre-delinquency, most of our recommendations in the previous chapters would be applicable. The only difference would be one of degree and emphasis. The pre-delinquent, as opposed to the occasional offender for example, is often in more need of a vigorous athletic and physical education program as an outlet for his over-aggressive tendencies. The physical education instructor and the coaches should be alerted to this need. In the case of a boy, individual attention should be given to developing his game skills so that he can find real satisfaction in sports. This may motivate him to improve his academic standing in order to earn varsity eligibility. Pre-delinquent girls can also profit from physical education and intra-mural sports. The modern dance, square dancing, and cheer-leading can sometimes be very helpful as well as arts, crafts, and music.

A warning word about vocational schools and industrial arts shops should be interposed here. There is no sense in using these places as dumping grounds for pre-delinquents and slow learners. Properly staffed and properly equipped, they are tremendously useful to youth and to the community—but they cannot function as miniature penal colonies any more than academic classrooms can. Every effort should be made to improve their status in this respect since one of their greatest handicaps is the social stigma attached to students who participate in their programs. It is true, of course, that many poorly adjusted boys find real meaning in a shop program. When they become catch-alls for problem cases, however, their usefulness is sharply reduced. Administrators with academic backgrounds are frequently guilty of poor judgment in this respect.

The parents of pre-delinquent youth must be prevailed upon to work closely with the school even if it means enlisting court support to obtain this cooperation. We shall discuss the importance of the family setting in the next chapter. It cannot be emphasized enough in the cases of pre-delinquents and delinquents.

We have repeatedly referred to the idea that the curriculum should fit the child, not vice versa. It is necessary to underline this concept in reference to pre-delinquents since this philosophy is absolutely fundamental in dealing with them. We cannot begin to make any progress if we are bound with concerns over standards of scholarship and school regulations relative to course content, sequence of courses, etc. The first business of the school in relation to the pre-delinquent child is to bring about a change of attitude—to open the door of hope. Once this has been accomplished, we can restore the normal application of rules and standards. As long as the school feels that it can do something for a child without referring him to another agency, it must be prepared to apply imagination, patience, and flexibility to the problem at hand.

Killing is against all the laws of God and man and yet, in time of war, many of us have been ordered to kill because we were defending our nation and our way of life. The battle against delinquency is war in a very real sense and unless we approximate the sense of urgency and mission of war we cannot hope to win.

13

The Influence of Family Life on School Discipline

Throughout this volume we have stressed the importance of finding the real causes of poor behavior. It is wiser to treat diseases than symptoms of diseases, but most school people are not trained for excursions into psychiatry and can only recommend appropriate referral for serious problems rooted in emotional disorder. Psychiatric practitioners are scarce except in large cities and emotional problems seem to be common. Fortunately most youngsters will respond to common sense and intelligent counseling that can be made available in any secondary school.

Practical educators know that many disciplinary problems of the school are really due to conditions in the students' homes. The family life of the student is far too important a factor in his behavior to be ignored, but the jurisdiction of the school is, and properly should be, limited by the traditional sanctity of the home. Officious meddling in home affairs by public employees is not an acceptable practice in a democratic society. Nor is it felt that the school should attempt to become all things to all people—to fill every vacuum in our society simply because it exists. The American public schools must belong to the people in fact as well as in theory, and its administrators do not have the right to move beyond the mandate of the people. This does not imply that public school leadership should merely follow the wishes of the most conservative elements of the community, but it does mean that any changes in the role of the school must be clearly defined and clearly accepted before they are put into practice. This is particularly true in matters affecting the family and the home.

HOME-SCHOOL PARTNERSHIP

The fact that most parents accept the necessity for cooperation between home and school is demonstrated by the strength and influence of parent-teacher associations, which cannot be accurately measured by attendance at meetings. American fathers may be reluctant to attend the monthly PTA meeting, but they accept the principles of the organization. Politicians are extremely loath to rouse the anger of these organizations, for example, by reckless cuts in school budgets. Above all, the American parent-teacher associations and parent-teacher-student associations are a tribute to the sincere concern of our nation for its youth and testimony to the proposition that the child is best served by close home-school cooperation. It is extremely frustrating for the school that this cooperation is readily offered by parents of children who create very little discipline trouble, but rather difficult to obtain where problems do exist.

Experienced teachers know that the emotional and social habits of youngsters are largely the result of family relationships and that it is the job of the parents to work toward a favorable environment in the home. They also know, however, that help and advice can only be offered when it is honestly desired, and even then with tact and understanding. Unfortunately, certain built-in misunderstandings between parents and teachers do exist. These cannot be ignored; for if they are exposed, they can be minimized and often completely overcome.

The influence of the home. Homes, like the people who live in them, are difficult to sort into pigeonholes for classification, but certain tendencies are quite common to the observer. Working closely with individual students, counselors and administrators find, with experience, certain patterns of home background emerging. However, one should avoid the pitfall of a hasty classification of a student's family life when working with him. Adolescents tend to take a good many favorable things for granted and to exaggerate annoyances. Unless the counselor or teacher has a clear reason for wanting the information, he should never encourage a student to criticize his home.

We cannot escape from the fact that the effect of the home is tremendous on such traits as honesty, conformity, and moral attitudes. Some knowledge of the nature of his family life is most helpful to an understanding of the student.

Broken homes are frequently singled out as very destructive forces in the life of a child. Sometimes we tend to oversimplify this factor and hastily conclude that if an outward break is prevented, everything will be all right. This simply does not work. A broken home, like alcoholism, is more of a symptom than a disease in itself. The underlying causes will probably persist even if the home is artificially glued together. Either way —openly or inwardly broken—this situation provides fertile soil for the growth of maladjustment in the child. The adults are usually emotionally out of balance to begin with, or have been disturbed by circumstances. They, in turn, project their basic instability into the children. Tension, discord, and conflict become common. Frequently the parents compete for the affection of the child, who wants to love them equally.

While it is perfectly true that many mothers are capable of raising their children successfully without a husband in the home, the school usually recognizes in the child the absence of strong male influence. If this can be partially compensated for by the friendly interest of a male teacher or counselor, so much the better. Children from homes dominated by adults of either sex frequently seek the influence of the opposite sex in their relatives, teachers, or adult friends. There is nothing abnormal about this; but when a teacher learns that he has been selected for this role by a student, he should proceed with caution so that he does not provide conflict in the student's mind through misunderstanding or lack of communication with the parent.

At some time or another, tension appears in every home. If either or both parents are given to frequent bursts of temper, this tension can be built up to a high level. Most children learn to accept these outbursts stoically, but heredity and environmental example being what they are, they frequently reflect these tendencies themselves—especially in adolescence. Stormy sessions in the home need not be unhealthy, since they do offer an escape valve for high pressure; but ground rules must be worked out by the combatants to avoid injuries or protracted sieges. Physical space, offering room for isolation or retreat, becomes important. One should never naively assume that love is not present simply because a husband and wife are shouting angry words at each other. They are simply indulging in the age-old marital privilege of blowing off steam. The school need only be concerned that the child learns to control his temper in school. This is not usually a serious problem, since the child, like his hot-tempered parent or parents, often feels that his temper explosions are his personal business—to be indulged in only in the sanctity of his home. When he cannot control himself in public by the time of adolescence, he very likely could benefit from psychiatric attention. Lacking this, the school can only provide isolation and sympathetic counseling when the outbursts occur.

The home in which one or both parents or the entire family were born and spent an appreciable length of time in another country is an interesting phenomenon on the American scene. There are certain possibilities for conflict with two sets of values and two cultures in somewhat turbulent conflict. There is a tendency for observers without first-hand experience to exaggerate this problem, however, and several recent surveys indicate that delinquency is less frequent in these homes than in native American homes.

In the early decades of the twentieth century, when masses of immigrants streamed through Ellis Island, we subscribed to the somewhat naive notion that America was a melting pot in which all these people would be boiled down into a stereotype of Uncle Sam. Their inferior foreign ways would be quickly discarded in favor of our vastly superior American ones. Such an attitude was bound to create family conflicts. Parents were heartsick at the changes they saw in their children. Children were embarrassed by their "greenhorn" parents. Little wonder that many of these homes were the scenes of adjustment difficulties.

Today we recognize the contributions of all these cultures to the American scene. Youngsters are encouraged to take pride in their dual heritage. They even feel that there is something very special in being an American by choice rather than accident of birth.

Families raised in the European (or Oriental) tradition are usually strong and closely knit. The father-image is a tower of strength upon which children can depend for security. Punishment is swift, fair, and certain, and parents substitute for psychology the accumulated wisdom of their race, often resulting in identical responses. Old values do not die easily and sometimes linger through several generations, particularly when conscious efforts are made to preserve old-world traditions.

The school usually has very little trouble with youngsters from immigrant homes, but administrators should be careful in contacting parents—especially in matters of discipline. Displeasure of school officials at the behavior of their children is considered a very serious matter and may lead to severe punishment even before all the facts are made clear.

The home that is heavily dominated by one of the parents, usually the father, presents a sharp conflict of values to the child who attends a school that attempts to operate in a democratic atmosphere. When strictness crosses the line into harshness and tyranny, it provokes fear, hatred, and feelings of guilt in the child, but little true respect for authority.

Unless the evidence clearly indicates unusual cruelty or brutality (which is *not necessarily synonymous* with autocracy in a home), the school can only attempt to offer a wholesome atmosphere to counterbalance that of the home. The American father still has the right to be the boss in his own home, even if television situation comedies have cast him as an ineffectual, bumbling clown.

Some homes are merely dormitories. Here there is a loose, anarchistic arrangement with no central figure of authority. Members of the family, like hotel occupants, go their separate ways and only come together now and then casually. The home becomes a dormitory, and the family a collection of individuals living at the same address.

Often a working mother and a father with two jobs set the stage for a home of this type. A home in which both parents work need not be a bad home; but when the mother's job is extremely demanding of her time or energy, her role as a mother will suffer. When a mother is unavailable at the times she is needed most, usually before and after school and at bedtime, a dangerous situation can develop. Material advantages are poor substitutes for a mother's stabilizing presence, and many youngsters drift into aimless and time-wasting habits because of lack of supervision. Even if they do not succumb to bad influences, their schoolwork suffers. The adolescent who can organize his time efficiently without adult assistance is rare indeed.

A working mother should consider both her tasks and arrange her time and efforts so that neither will suffer, but her primary responsibility must be her home and children. When she fails and her children begin to stray, the school's first duty is to keep her informed. An enforced conference which takes her away from her job can bring home dramatically to her the need for change before it is too late. The school can, of course, attempt to provide the needed guidance and direction, but it cannot hope to compensate for a non-functioning mother.

The influence of economic status. Extreme poverty can be a deteriorating influence in the life of a child, particularly in an urban area. Except in times of prolonged depression or in areas where unemployment is widespread and prolonged, extreme poverty is generally associated with people who are inadequate in one or more ways. Men who cannot find jobs when work is plentiful are not often the best fathers. The results are quite familiar—large families, dirty and cramped homes, poor supervision of children and low moral standards. Life becomes an uphill struggle for children brought up in these homes, and the ones who rise above their surroundings are often very superior people. Unless outside influences like settlement houses or schools can reach them soon enough, they may elect to drift with the dreary currents of the only life they know. When a child must learn to steal or go hungry, be aggressive or be beaten, he does not enter adolescence very responsive to the values taught by the school.

Schools serving urban slum areas have a very special duty to salvage these children and to show them that there is meaning to the American dream. Often these schools must fill many gaps in the lives of the children if the latter are to have any hope of success. Needless to say, such schools need the best teachers, the best equipment, and the complete cooperation of the community. Too often in the past, they have not had them, but we cannot continue to pay lip service to equality of opportunity and continue this neglect.

Economic insecurity is not only a problem in slum areas. It affects every family which lives beyond its income regardless of the size of that income. It breeds conflict and insecurity, and has a very bad effect on growing children. In addition to shaking their security when they need it most, it sets a poor example and encourages the adoption of dubious values.

The school can do a great deal to counteract economic irresponsibility by teaching courses or units in consumer education, and by constantly encouraging desirable goals in life. It often seems like an uphill struggle, but most of our young people graduate from high school with a normal, healthy outlook on life. Our schools cannot take all the credit, but they should be granted their share.

PARENT-SCHOOL RELATIONS

The school is responsible for maintaining two-way channels of communication between teachers and parents. The need becomes dramatically obvious when serious discipline problems occur, but it is also a very effective way to prevent trouble. Every effort must be made to overcome conflicts between home and school and to minimize their built-in misunderstandings mentioned earlier in this chapter. A first step might be to analyze the causes for some of these misunderstandings.

Reasons for home-school conflict.

1. *There is a serious lack of information for the public.* The school cannot expect average parents to go out of their way to seek information about the schools. Their usual source is the child, and that source can certainly not be relied upon for

the complete picture. Every possible medium of information must be used. Regular newsletters, sent by mail rather than by students, can be very effective if they are well written and carefully edited. P.T.A. units are usually very happy to underwrite the cost of these publications if they can include their own publicity and meeting notices.

2. *Parents tend to view teachers as not completely normal human beings.* Undoubtedly they are influenced by the stereotyped teacher so often portrayed in fiction and drama as a stiff-necked spinster (male or female!) devoid of most human attributes. Perhaps they feel that people who dedicate themselves to lives of genteel poverty by choice must be a little strange.

In any event, the burden of proof is on the teacher to prove that he is a human being not unlike the parent. The teacher must, in other words, get used to the idea that he is a victim of prejudice.

3. *Teachers have prejudices too.* Many of them view parents as people who know little or nothing about child raising or education but who have far too much influence with school boards. Sometimes they actually fear this influence, although tenure laws should have eliminated this fear in all but the most timid. Thus, the meeting of parent and teacher can be a meeting of two people with serious prejudices against each other before they begin to talk. The teacher can do a great deal to overcome this hurdle by making a serious and intelligent effort to overcome his own prejudice and by being aware of the parent as a human being.

4. *Unmarried teachers find it difficult really to understand how parents feel about their children.* On the other hand, these teachers can be more objective in viewing the child. This disadvantage and its compensating advantage should be recognized and acknowledged by both parent and teacher.

5. *Parents have a tendency to think of schools in terms of*

the schools they attended. This can only be counteracted by information and yet more information.

Resolving misunderstandings. The principal is the key figure in the efforts to obtain optimum home and school cooperation. In this as in so many other matters, he must set the tone. Teachers should feel that he will support them when parents become unreasonable. Parents should feel that he is truly concerned with the welfare of their children and nor merely in "covering" for the faculty whether they are right or wrong. He walks a difficult path.

We have pointed out the obvious fact that courtesy and friendliness on the part of the teacher can overcome a great many misunderstandings. In addition to this, the teacher can be made aware of certain common-sense rules for discussing difficult situations with parents. Here is a suggested check-list which might be useful in preparing for such an interview.

1. *Permit the parent to release his emotions by stating his position first.* Do not interrupt until he has finished. This will take self discipline, but it is extremely beneficial to the successful conduct of the ensuing conference. Pent-up emotions have a tendency to strangle objectivity.

2. *Emphasize objective data.* Bring to the conference all pertinent data such as your class record book, significant test papers, etc. Remember that most of the information the parent has comes from the student's highly subjective reports. Parents should be aware that some subjective judgments must enter into evaluation, but they are usually unhappy about the idea. They will accept the evidence of poor grades when the child has simply failed to retain factual knowledge, but they are loath to accept negative reports on his general understandings and his attitude. They often prefer to think that the teacher fails to understand *him.*

3. *Keep the conference focused on the student and his ultimate goals.* Parents frequently prefer to concentrate on what *they* expect of their children and what *they* think the children can achieve.

4. *Keep the conference goal centered and guided back from extraneous excursions to the business at hand—how the parent and the teacher can work together for the welfare of the child.*

5. *Stress the importance of the total picture rather than the immediate problem.* This is not to say that the latter should be avoided, but no minor problem should be permitted to monopolize such a valuable opportunity to create partnership out of misunderstanding. Settle the issue with facts and figures and then place it in its true perspective.

6. *Be positive.* No matter how bad the student is doing, there must be something good to say about him. Say it. Then move on to positive recommendations rather than dwelling on his shortcomings. Let the facts speak for themselves on the negative aspects.

There is entirely too much at stake when parent meets teacher to permit personal pride and human weaknesses to throw the relationship out of focus. The teacher is not merely meeting another adult socially. It does not matter whether he likes the parent or not. It does not matter whether wide differences of temperament, intelligence, social class, or personality stand in the way of rapport. The teacher is doing a professional job for which he is being paid. The physician does not necessarily like all of his patients and the lawyer most certainly cannot like all of his clients. It is the teacher's professional duty to establish a working relationship with the home in the best interests of the *student.*

One could go on for some time listing the handicaps and difficulties encountered daily in the operation of our secondary schools. Certainly not the least of these is the uncooperative parent. Every effort made to strengthen the ties between home and school are well worth while, not only in terms of improving discipline but as a way of increasing the overall effectiveness of the entire school program.

14

Securing Community Support Is Essential

It has been our point of view throughout this volume that teamwork in the wake of intelligent, professional leadership is the key to sound disciplinary policies and procedures in secondary education. This teamwork, as our recommendations have indicated, must extend the school into the community it serves, and the resultant relationship between school and community is so important that it deserves thorough analysis.

THE SECONDARY SCHOOL AND THE COMMUNITY

America's secondary schools did not always truly belong to their communities. The early academies and the first public high schools located in the larger cities were remote institutions surrounded, figuratively at least, by walls which separated them from their surroundings. Gradually the walls began to crumble and in the early decades of the twentieth century the schools began an effort to enlist the support of their communities.

After World War II the schools found themselves caught up in the rapid and far-reaching changes which resulted in making the community-school a reality. Even the buildings were constructed so that their facilities could be used for a variety of adult activities when school was not in session. Part of the reason for this multiple use of school plant was the high cost of construction which awakened the public to the need for more efficient use of facilities, but the real driving force behind school and community integration was the growing realization on the part of school administrators that schools could not remain effective if they were isolated from the people who support them.

All of this had a very real and direct bearing on school discipline. Community interest and involvement has a close relationship to the adequacy of financial support, and dollars *can* buy quality—even in education. From proper support we obtain superior teaching, sound leadership, adequate facilities, and a meaningful curriculum, all of which are essential to effective discipline.

From another point of view, school discipline is tied to the community even more closely. Secondary school students reflect the behavior patterns of the entire community. Youngsters tend to be like their environment and any effort to improve their behavior must involve an improvement in the total environment. The school located in a slum cannot hope for an appreciable improvement in the attitudes and behavior of its students unless conditions in the slum area itself are improved. The school which serves a wealthy suburb cannot hope to win the battle against materialistic thinking and snobbery while these evils are firmly entrenched in the community itself. While there has been a renewal of interest in the point of view popular in the twenties that the schools should take the lead in reconstructing society, the strength of the conservative view that the schools exist to perpetuate the *status quo* shows no signs of being broken. It seems futile to perpetuate this artificial dichotomy when there is so much to be done. We *all* need to get busy on reconstructing society by reviving lasting values.

It is later than we think and there is no time for quibbling about procedure.

Closer school-community integration can also pay rich dividends in more effective cooperation between the school and other agencies, employers, homes, and religious institutions in matters concerning opportunities for individual students. The school, acting as coordinator, can obtain for the pupil the right services at the right time without duplication of efforts.

Community schools often enrich the curriculum by using the community as a laboratory. Industry, business, town government, public utilities, libraries, museums, and the people themselves become sources of information within a planned program that is not to be confused with some form of extracurricular activity. The actual classroom becomes more of a center of operations than a locus of all learning. Guided tours are conducted, meetings are held, speakers are brought in to school. All of this can be, and has been, accomplished without any sacrifice of fundamental material or orderly sequence of presentation if a few common-sense rules are observed: (1) Careful planning, both long and short term, must precede all learning experiences—in or out of the classroom, (2) All learning must be preceded by motivational introduction and followed by summary and evaluation, (3) All out-of-school experiences should be previewed by the teacher, (4) All laymen involved must be completely willing to cooperate, (5) The out-of-school experiences must be worth the inconvenience in terms of more effective learning. They cannot be justified merely as diversions or even as "good public relations." They must stand on their own feet as sound *educational* practices.

THE TEACHER IN THE COMMUNITY

The community school idea is a two-way street which also means that teachers and administrators must become closely identified with the life of the community. This has not always been a common practice. From earliest Colonial days until the period following World War II teachers have occupied a peculiar position in American communities. With the exception of those who were born and brought up in the towns wherein they served, teachers were seldom integrated into their communities. They were with them but not of them. Their roles began and ended in the school and out of the classroom they were generally regarded as nonentities.

The reasons for this were many, most of them rooted in insecurity of position and inadequate salaries. With some justification, most people considered the teaching profession to be made up largely of unsaleable men and unmarriageable women who were content to occupy economic and social positions inferior to others of comparable education. In one respect they were not ignored—they were carefully watched to see that they conformed to the behavioral code of the most conservative groups in the community.

World War II and its immediate aftermath saw a real crisis developing in the teaching profession with thousands of teachers, mostly men, leaving their classrooms for good. It is commonly felt that the first postwar decade saw the low point in American education. Then, suddenly, the face of America changed and exciting things began to happen. Migration out of the cities into the suburbs and from region to region created new communities and reshaped old ones. Birthrates continued to climb. The already threatening shortage of classrooms became acute. Always responsive to a first-class crisis, America began to move. Mass communication media discovered the crisis and began to publicize it. Politicians became concerned. But the backbone of the movement to improve the schools was found among the new, young families of suburbia. Angered when the welfare of their children was threatened, they made it very clear that they were not interested in excuses. They wanted good teachers and good schools and proceeded to go about getting them!

From this point on the downward trend reversed itself and American public education began to move in the right direction. Increasing numbers of able young people were attracted to teaching and the American teacher emerged in a new image. No longer satisfied with starvation wages and inferior social status, and with no intention of conforming to a stuffy code of behavior, the new teacher took for granted complete acceptance as a member of the community, and he usually found it. Although the decade of the fifties did not see a complete change in the status of the teacher, especially in terms of salary, the improvements were so dramatic and far-reaching that they could not help but inspire the entire profession.

All these changes in the educational climate saw a new role developing for the teacher in the community. Civic organizations and even political parties opened their doors to teachers. No longer were educators limited to youth leadership roles in the Boy Scouts, Girl Scouts, etc. The public began to understand that teachers who worked with children all day might prefer to associate with adults in their off-duty time. In these associations with influential adults the teachers found an opportunity to interpret informally to them the program of the schools. Their very presence as normal, intelligent adults helped to break down old prejudices and old misconceptions of the teacher image.

Teachers' unions and associations also learned that they had to assume the responsibilities of *community service organizations* if they were to maintain their effectiveness in fighting for better salaries and better schools. Nothing can be quite as injurious to school public relations as the teachers' organization that is only heard from when a question of teachers' salaries is pending. While it is true that a good salary battle is more interesting to the press than routine service functions such as the awarding of scholarships, etc., the teachers' organization should take steps to maintain close relationships with newspapers, radio stations, and television stations so that their service functions receive a reasonable amount of attention. In many larger school systems these organizations have hired paid secretaries, at least on a part-time basis, to supervise public relations along with other duties.

The teacher in his role as a citizen would do well to counteract the impression that his only community interest is the school system. Those of us who work in the schools are probably convinced that education is the most important single responsibility of the community—but we must remain aware of the fact that it is not the only one. Other services are important too and neglecting them can affect the schools. In order to provide a sound tax base to support schools it is usually essential to attract industry to the community. Industry wants good schools for the children of its employees but it must also have adequate sewer and water services, good roads, and police and fire protection—all within the framework of a reasonable tax rate. Sometimes compromises are necessary in order to serve the best interests of the entire community. Teachers who create the impression that they are blind to the total picture and interested only in the welfare of the school system lose their effectiveness as leaders in the community. There may be truth in the familiar slogan "Good schools make good communities," but there is also a suspicion of overstatement if we expect this sweeping promise to mean that a properly supported school system can, by itself, improve a poor community overnight. Would it not be more realistic to suggest that "Good communities need good schools," if we must go to the public with pithy slogans?

In this volume, we are specifically concerned with good discipline, one of the by-products of a good school system.

Poor citizenship and delinquency cannot be treated as a disease that only infects secondary school youngsters or any given age group. Its causes and consequences affect every citizen in the community. Its roots are everywhere—in the crowded tenements, in the dirty streets, in the inadequate social agencies and recreational facilities, and in the general moral tone of the community. The teen age population is a mirror in which the community can see itself as it really is—not as it thinks it should look. Any program for improvement must involve all of us, not merely the youngsters who reflect our shortcomings.

COMMUNITY ACTION FOR CITIZENSHIP IMPROVEMENT

Here are a few specific recommendations for improvements which can be made in eight areas of community life. They involve all of us and cannot be made without the cooperation and help of all of us.

Political organizations. The weakness in our democratic structure at the level of town and city government is well known and one of the reasons for it is rather simple to state: Able people do not make themselves available for elective offices in sufficient numbers. The result is that school board memberships and town and city council memberships go by default to inadequate persons. This creates a climate favorable to politicking in its meanest sense and discourages capable administrators from serving the town or city. The result is inefficiency, waste, and sometimes corruption. This sets up a vicious circle. Cheap politics discourages participation by capable citizens which, in turn, perpetuates the cheap politics. Leadership is a precious commodity. It must be actively sought after—not taken for granted. Reform movements and "good government" tickets in local elections are very desirable, but they are usually created around a temporary situation and they have a tendency to burn out rather quickly when public apathy reappears. What is needed is a sustained drive to enlist the participation of educated, intelligent people in the regular political parties. This is a frustrating process since they are not always truly welcome, but the moral and ethical tone of the community cannot rise much above the level of those who serve in elective offices. The best school systems can quickly decay under the pressures of patronage and low level politics.

Law enforcement. A professional police force, reasonably free of political interference and intelligently administered, is essential to a good community. This cannot be accomplished in an atmosphere of patronage and penny pinching. Ticket fixing, pay-offs, and favored treatment to individuals with influence sets the worst possible example for youth. Confused by the double standards of adults, many of them will accept the petty corruption they see around them as the norm rather than the idealistic images created in their civics classes.

Competent and understanding juvenile officers and probation counselors are invaluable to the disciplinary officials of the school. Working together and freely exchanging information they can sometimes accomplish miracles with maladjusted youngsters in and out of school. The school should not hesitate to seek this cooperation actively. The teacher as a citizen should not hesitate to lend his support to the police department in its constant struggle for adequate equipment and salaries. An effective police department will make his work easier by improving citizenship standards in the entire community.

Housing. Slum clearance, urban renewal, revision of antiquated zoning laws and building codes, and a close check on the operations of slum landlords, are all essential to community improvement. In recent years we have witnessed many well-intentioned but unintelligent attempts to solve the slum problem by merely tearing down old buildings and replacing them with barracks-like projects. No more planning has been involved than in moving a cat and her kittens from a dirty box into a clean one. People are not kittens. Some of these projects carry built-in guarantees that they will remain slums by reason of a maximum income requirement for residency that continues to drive out the potential community leaders within the project. What remains is an artificial community consisting only of the families of inadequate wage earners. Our social scientists and architects know how to deal with these problems of public housing, but it is necessary to apply the findings of their study and research in the planning.

Many communities have obtained excellent results in controlling the future of housing by involving school administrators and many other municipal authorities together with professional planners, financial institutions, and builders in projecting long-range plans for community development. Blighted neighborhoods and slums usually got that way through lack of planning and coordination. There is nothing mutually exclusive between private enterprise and community planning. On the contrary, nations living under free enterprise have a *far* better record of providing decent housing for their people than nations under communism. America's failures in housing have resulted from too little intelligent planning and community control rather than from too much.

Recreation. Prolonged material prosperity and the shortening of the work week have brought into focus the need for increased recreational opportunities for people of all ages. Most of our efforts in this direction have been expended in providing wholesome recreation for children and youth and the results indicate that we have only scratched the surface. Our usual justification for the expenditure of tax money for recreational facilities is that it will cut down on juvenile delinquency. Perhaps this is the most effective way to obtain funds from reluctant officials, but we should not attempt to overstate this claim. The allocation of a few thousand dollars for recreation will not stamp out delinquency. To claim that it will is dangerous nonsense that may endanger the future support of a sensible program of recreation. No matter how adequate the program may be, it cannot help youngsters who do not choose to participate, and delinquent youngsters are not often attracted to the adult-supervised recreation programs—they prefer something more lurid and dangerous.

This is not to say that recreation does not contribute to the battle against delinquency, particularly among the younger children who may be vulnerable to bad influences. A consistent, professionally coordinated, and adequately supported recreation program will most certainly help to raise the standards of citizenship among youth but the real benefits will come only after several years of operation—this is no rapid-fire panacea for all our social ills.

Employment opportunities. If play is important to youth, so is work. Job opportunities, both part-time and full-time, are of tremendous importance in building character, maturity, and self esteem in young people whether they come from tenements or mansions. Every young American is entitled to the unique satisfaction of being paid for his labor early in life. Prolonged periods of depression such as the decade of the thirties are ruinous to human beings in many ways besides merely creating want. There is a sickness of the soul that comes with prolonged unemployment—a cruel disease that destroys the faith of the individual in himself and his nation. Economic adjustments resulting from automation in industry, regional shifts of large industries, depletion of certain natural resources, etc. often bring widespread unemployment to specific areas even in times of general national prosperity. While these problems are more effectively handled at the state and federal level, the local community must take a good deal of initiative in helping itself. Realistic steps must be taken toward the goal of attracting diversified business and industry to the community not only to provide tax dollars but, more importantly, to provide jobs.

Intelligent and far-sighted planning is as important in this area as it is in projecting future housing patterns for the community. People must have jobs to pay for their houses and youth must have jobs or they will either leave the community or remain to decay.

The secondary school, as we have pointed out, can help its students to prepare for and to find employment by maintaining close contacts with business and industry. This effort can be amply justified if for no other reason than as an effort to combat delinquency. There is still a good deal of truth in the ancient Calvinist idea that Satan finds work for idle hands.

Community agencies. In terms of numbers America has no lack of agencies concerned with the welfare and health of the people. Public and private agencies exist at every level, often competing vigorously for tax and gift support and even for clients. Clubs and service organizations dabble now and then in welfare work, some of them in an extremely generous way. There is no mistaking America's generosity toward the less fortunate, but there is a great deal of room for improvement in the way of organization and coordination.

We would urge our citizens to concern themselves with the following improvements in agency structure:

1. We must provide community coordination to avoid competition, overlapping, and waste. The administration of welfare is a complicated business and requires the overall supervision of trained professionals to eliminate waste and inefficiency. There is simply no excuse for agency competition when there is so much to be done.

2. We must provide for an effective exchange of information to avoid senseless duplication of effort.

3. Schools should concentrate agency liaison in the hands of one person, preferably a trained counselor, to avoid the neces-

sity of attempting to do things within the school that community agencies are willing and able to do better.

4. Far greater efforts should be expended to obtain psychiatric and psychological services for those who need them and cannot afford to pay or those who do not know how to obtain them. Referral and diagnosis are especially important since many people who need this sort of help are either unaware of their need or unwilling to face the fact of their need.

5. Athletic programs for early adolescents and pre-adolescents should have professional direction to avoid the pitfalls of (a) expending the greatest efforts on the natural athletes who need it least and (b) failing to develop the talents of average and below average youngsters because of intense pressures to produce winning teams.

6. We must renew our efforts to coordinate fund drives for agencies. The public is becoming increasingly disenchanted with multiple requests for funds and may fail to respond to the most deserving drives if the constant appeals continue. Distasteful as it may seem, some form of governmental regulation may be necessary to preserve the effectiveness of voluntary giving.

Adult education. Adult Education programs have increased tremendously in popularity in the past few years. Although most of it has been recreational and hobby centered, a good deal of it has been of some academic stature. We would urge the administrators to increase their efforts to build interest in courses concerned with improving the skills of citizenship and parenthood. It would also be of great advantage to introduce material which interprets the program of the schools. Admittedly, courses of this type are not very popular with the people who need them most, but this is no reason to give up attempts. Special, short-term courses centered around specific problems and taught with skill and imagination should have appeal.

School public relations. So much has been said about "selling" our schools that we will not attempt a detailed treatment at this point. We would urge briefly, however, that school administrators avoid the tendency to imitate the methods of Madison Avenue. We cannot make up for past bungling of public relations by high pressure programs which gloss over our shortcomings and exaggerate the significance of our successes. The story needs to be told honestly and simply. The public is entitled to know exactly what is going on in our schools and exactly what we intend to do in the future. We cannot gamble on the confidence of the people.

Here is the key to the future of American public education—the confidence and the concern of the people. It cannot be repeated too often that our schools are as good or as bad as we want them to be. Cults and fads may come and go, crisis and resultant concern may be followed by apathy and mediocrity, but one thing remains constant—quality follows sustained support and sustained support calls for sustained efforts from all of us to keep the schools close to the community.

Index